Be My Guest

generations of family cooking

By Suellen Kruse and Priscilla K. van Horne

Be My Guest

A savory dinner is an expression of love. Love of people, love of food, sharing with friends, — all is expressed when you invite guests to your home. The home is an expression of personality, so too is the table setting which greets your guests. Color is important on the table and in the food served. Eye appeal is so important to make eating pleasurable. So Be My Guest is written to suggest combinations of foods that will be attractive and tasty.

We dedicate this book in loving memory of our mother,

Evelyn Kruse Kurtz (1910-2003)

Dedication

She was born in Minneapolis, Minnesota and lived there all of her life. She married at the young age of nineteen just before the Great Depression. She learned to cook mostly by trial and error with some help from her mother-in-law. As youngsters we lived in the country outside of Minneapolis. Our father planted a big hobby garden every spring and he also raised chickens. Mother canned lots of vegetables and fruits and made jams and jellies. We had a fruit cellar in the basement of our home where all this food was stored.

Our mother was a wonderful cook. She described herself as an ordinary cook, but there was nothing ordinary about the meals she prepared. She had a good sense of "design", so when it came to food, she had a talent for planning menus and using flavors, colors and textures to make food look appealing as well as being tasty. Throughout our childhood, she cooked delectable meals, and our family always ate dinner together at the dining room table.

Mother belonged to a group of young women who called themselves "The Sandwich Club". In those days no one had much money so their monthly meetings were held in someone's home, and they each brought a sandwich. All the food was combined on a large platter and everyone shared. The hostess provided coffee and dessert. When they got together they talked about many subjects including parenting, recipes and handwork ideas. All of the women were good cooks and many of Mother's favorite recipes came from these friends. They stayed together for sixty years and remained close. All are now deceased, but some of their recipes live on in this cookbook.

Food is a common thread in our family memories. Mother loved to entertain, so she and Dad had Christmas parties, Easter brunches and New Year's Eve parties as well as many, many Sunday dinners for our family and relatives.

She showed her love for all of us through her cooking. It was in her later years that she wanted to write a cookbook and share some of her favorite recipes. She began to select recipes and file them by subject in separate folders. She named the book "Be My Guest", which was a fitting title for a woman who used her culinary talents to nurture others. She also wrote the introduction and three of the chapter prefaces which have been reproduced in Mother's handwriting. As time went on, she became unable to finish the project. It was our wish to finish it for her, and we added some of our own favorites. We are sure you will enjoy this book.

Suellen Kruse and Priscilla K. van Horne

First Edition: November 2007
Printed in the USA by Pro Print, Duluth Minnesota

ISBN 978-0-9798231-0-7

Authors, Evelyn Kruse Kurtz, Suellen Kruse and Priscilla K.van Horne
Karl Hansen — computer guru
Katherine Hellner — graphic designer
Jen van Horne — editor-proof reading
Marie Sweeney — watercolor artist — front cover
Donna Williams — index specialist

For more information go to www.kahneetah.com

Be My Guest

TABLE OF CONTENTS

Appetizers and Beverages..... 1 - 17

Soups.................................... 18 - 33

Salads and Salad Dressings... 34 - 62

Egg Dishes............................ 63 - 75

Fish and Sea Food................ 76 - 85

Main Dishes.......................... 86 - 123

Vegetables & Side Dishes...... 124 - 147

Potatoes and Rice................. 148 - 155

Breads and Rolls.................. 156 - 167

Cookies and Bars.................. 168 - 186

Desserts................................ 187 - 220

Miscellaneous........................ 221 - 228

Index.....................................230 - 233

1 Appetizers and Beverages

Appetizers are teasers. If they are imaginative and intriguing, your guests or "audience" eagerly await the next act. Whatever is served should not be too rich or heavy to take pleasure from what is to follow. Some suggestions follow that have been rewarded with applause.

Artichoke Bars

2 (6 oz.) jars marinated artichoke hearts
1 large onion, chopped
1 clove garlic, minced
4 eggs
½ cup soft breadcrumbs
½ tsp. salt
Freshly ground pepper
½ tsp. oregano
Dash of Tabasco
½ lb. sharp Cheddar cheese, grated
Handful of minced parsley

Preheat oven to 325°. Drain marinade from one jar of artichoke hearts into skillet. Drain other jar and discard marinade. Sauté onion and garlic in reserved marinade until it is limp; remove from heat. Chop the drained artichoke hearts. In a bowl, beat the eggs. Add crumbs, salt, pepper, oregano, Tabasco, cheese, parsley, artichoke hearts and sautéed onion and garlic; combine well. Turn mixture into buttered 7 x 11 inch pan. Bake at 325° for 30 minutes or until set. Cool slightly and cut into small squares. Serve warm or at room temperature. Can be made and frozen. Thaw and reheat before serving.

Makes 18 squares.

Artillery Punch

1 cup sugar
Juice of 6 lemons
2 tbsp. Angostura bitters
1 qt. claret wine
1 qt. sherry
1 qt. rye, bourbon or scotch whisky
1 qt. brandy
1 qt. club soda

Combine sugar and lemon juice and stir well. Add rest of ingredients, except club soda,and mix well. Pour over a block of ice in punch bowl and add club soda.

Serves 20.

Avocado Cream Cheese Spread

1 (8 oz.) pkg. cream cheese, softened
1 ripe avocado, cubed
Lemon juice
Salt
Onion juice to taste

Combine all ingredients carefully so as not to crush cubed avocado. Refrigerate to blend flavors, but bring to room temperature before serving. Good with Fritos or tortilla chips

Bourbon Hot Dogs

1 cup catsup
½ cup brown sugar
½ cup bourbon
1 lb. hot dogs

Cut hot dogs into bite size pieces. Mix catsup, brown sugar and bourbon. Put hot dogs in casserole and pour sauce over. Mix well. Bake at 350° for 1 ½ hours, stirring every 20 minutes. Serve with toothpicks.

Cheese Mushroom Royale Appetizer

8-12 oz. fresh mushrooms, finely chopped
2 tbsp. margarine
½ tsp. garlic salt
2 tbsp. green onions, chopped, 4 or more
1 tsp. lemon juice
1 tsp. Worcestershire sauce
1 (8 oz.) pkg. crescent rolls
2 (3 oz.) pkgs. cream cheese, very soft
¼ cup Parmesan, grated

Sauté mushrooms in margarine. Add onions and sauté. Add garlic salt, lemon juice and Worcestershire. Cook until liquid is evaporated. Pat crescent roll dough in a greased 9 x 13 pan, covering bottom and ¼ inch up the sides. Spread cream cheese over the dough. Add mushroom mixture and sprinkle with Parmesan. Bake at 350° for 20 minutes. Cut into squares.

Makes 32 squares.

Children's Punch

1 qt. cranberry juice
1 (6 oz.) can frozen orange concentrate
1 (6 oz.) can frozen lemonade
1 (48 oz.) can pineapple juice
1 qt. ginger ale
Frozen cherries and pineapple tidbits

Combine fruit juices. Add ginger ale. Pour over an ice ring in punch bowl that contains frozen cherries and pineapple tidbits.

Makes 30 (4 oz.) servings.

Crab Canapés

2 ½ dozen 2" bread rounds from thinly sliced bread
Melted butter
1 (5 oz.) can crabmeat
½ cup cream of mushroom soup, undiluted
2 tbsp. sherry
1 tbsp. chopped pimento
¼ tsp. salt
Tabasco, a few drops
Cheddar cheese, grated

Brush bread rounds with butter and heat in slow oven 225°, for 1 hour. Combine all other ingredients except cheese. Spread crab mixture on bread rounds. Top with cheese and broil 2 - 3 minutes.

Makes 30 appetizers.

Fantastic Stuff

Fantastic to put on crackers and serve as an hors d' oeuvre

1 (1 lb.) eggplant
¼ cup olive oil
½ cup Bermuda onion, thinly sliced
½ cup tomato sauce
½ cup celery, finely diced
2 tsp. capers, chopped
8-10 stuffed green olives, sliced
2 tbsp. wine vinegar
1 tsp. salt and 1 tsp. pepper, used sparingly
½ tsp. garlic powder

Peel and dice eggplant into small pieces. Heat oil on moderate heat. Add eggplant and cook 10 minutes or until soft. Stir often. Remove eggplant and mash it. Set aside. Add onion to pan and cook 10 minutes until brown (add more oil if necessary). Add tomato sauce and celery and cook until tender. Add capers, olives, eggplant, vinegar, salt, pepper and garlic powder. Reduce heat to low and simmer 20 minutes. Cool and chill until ready to serve. Should be served chilled for best taste.

Enough for 40 crackers.

Fish House Punch

Delicious, but POTENT

9 lemons
9 oranges
1 fifth light rum
½ of a fifth of dark rum
½ of a fifth of brandy
1 cup apricot brandy
1 ¼ cups simple syrup
1 qt. of water, plain or sparkling

Make simple syrup by combining 1 ¼ cups water and 1 ¼ cups sugar. Boil 5 minutes and cool. Squeeze oranges and lemons. Refrigerate juices and simple syrup. At serving time, put juices and syrup in a punch bowl. Add liquor and let mellow an hour over a block of ice or ice ring. Add sparkling water. Serve in punch cups.

Serves 12 - 15.

Hot Artichoke Spread

1 (14 oz.) can artichoke hearts, drained and finely chopped
1 cup mayonnaise
6 - 8 oz. Parmesan, freshly grated
6 oz. Monterey Jack cheese, chunked and stirred in
Dash of Cayenne pepper
Dash of Tabasco *(more if desired)*
Salt to taste

Mix all together and bake at 350º for 30 minutes.
Serve warm with crackers.

Serves 15.

Hot Cheese Spread

¾ cup Cheddar cheese, grated
¾ cup Swiss cheese, grated
1 cup pitted ripe olives, chopped
1 cup onion, chopped
1 cup mayonnaise

Mix all and heat in a shallow baking dish at 350º for 30 minutes.
Serve with assorted crisp crackers.

Hot Crabmeat Spread

12 oz. cream cheese
1 can crabmeat
2 tbsp. mayonnaise
2 tsp. horseradish
Salt and pepper
Chopped chives

Soften cream cheese and drain crabmeat. Mix all and bake at 325°
for 45 minutes. Serve with assorted crackers.

Serves 8.

Hot Mushroom Dip

4 slices bacon
½ lb. fresh mushrooms, sliced
1 medium onion, finely chopped
1 clove garlic, minced
2 tbsp. flour
Pepper
1 (8 oz.) pkg. cream cheese, cut into small pieces
2 tsp. Worcestershire
2 tsp. soy sauce
½ cup sour cream

Fry bacon until crisp. Drain; saving 2 tbsp. drippings in skillet. Crumble bacon and set aside. Add mushrooms, onion and garlic to drippings and cook over medium heat until tender and most of mushroom liquid has evaporated, about 6 - 8 minutes. Mix in flour and pepper. Add cream cheese, Worcestershire and soy sauce. Reduce heat to low and stir until cheese is melted. Remove from heat. Stir in sour cream and bacon. Serve warm with assorted crackers and breadsticks.

Makes 2 ½ - 3 cups.

Mexican Fudge Appetizer

8 oz. Cheddar cheese, shredded
8 oz. Monterey Jack, shredded
3 eggs, beaten with a fork
½ jar medium salsa

Combine and pour into an 8 x 8 ungreased pan. Bake at 350º for 20 minutes. Cut into small squares and put each one on a plain round tortilla chip or round cracker. Serve warm or at room temperature.

Mother's Dill Dip

1 cup sour cream
1 cup mayonnaise
1 tbsp. dill weed
1 tbsp. parsley flakes
1 tbsp. Beau Monde seasoning
1 tbsp. onion juice or grated onion

Combine all ingredients and chill until ready to serve with veggies or chips.

Enough for a party.

Open House Punch

1 fifth Southern Comfort
3 qts. 7 UP
6 oz. fresh lemon juice
1 (6 oz.) can frozen orange juice
1 (6 oz.) can frozen lemonade
Orange and lemon slices

Chill ingredients. Mix in punch bowl, 7 UP last. Add drops of red food coloring if desired. Stir. Add ice and orange and lemon slices.

Serves 32.

Peanut Butter and Chutney Canapés

Men love these and they are so easy!

White bread cut into 2" rounds or cut into 4 strips per slice
Peanut butter
Major Grey's chutney
Bacon, fried crisp and crumbled

Toast bread on one side, lightly (in oven at 225º). Turn bread over and spread with peanut butter. Put a layer of chutney on top and then bacon. Put under broiler and broil 2 - 3 minutes.

Pecan Stuffed Mushrooms

14 - 16 large mushroom caps
4 tbsp. butter
4 green onions, finely chopped
1 cup soft bread crumbs
4 tbsp. bacon, cooked crisp and crumbled
2 tbsp. chopped pecans
2 tbsp. sherry
4 - 6 tbsp. sour cream

Wash mushroom caps and remove stems. Place on paper towel to dry. In a heavy skillet, melt butter and sauté onions about 3 minutes. Remove from heat and stir in bread crumbs, bacon and pecans. Add sherry and enough sour cream to make a fluffy mixture. Stuff the mushrooms, heaping the stuffing. Bake at 400º about 20 minutes until heated through.

Makes 14 - 16 mushrooms.

Priscilla's Clam Dip

2 (8 oz.) pkgs. cream cheese at room temperature
¼ lb. butter, melted
2 cans minced clams, drained
2 (7 oz.) cans mushrooms, drained
2 tbsp. dried onion, rehydrated

Mix all and heat on stove on low heat. Transfer to chafing dish. Serve with a variety of crackers.

Ruth's Daiquiri

2 (6 oz.) cans frozen lemonade
1 (6 oz.) can frozen limeade
3 cans water
1 fifth light rum

Mix and put in freezer or refrigerator.

Sangria

1 bottle red wine (Burgundy for example)
½ cup sugar
½ cup lemon juice
1 orange and 1 lemon, thinly sliced
1 oz. Arrow Triple Sec
1 oz. brandy
1 (7 oz.) bottle chilled club soda

Combine all except club soda and fruit and chill.
Add club soda and fruit just before serving.

Serves 8.

Sauce Iberia Dip

1 cup mayonnaise
½ tsp. dry mustard
¼ tsp. garlic salt
1 tbsp. anchovy paste
½ tsp. Tabasco
2 tbsp. tarragon vinegar
1 tsp. parsley, chopped
3 tbsp. stuffed olives, finely chopped
3 tbsp. sweet pickles, chopped
1 tsp. onion, chopped
3 hard cooked eggs, finely chopped

Blend all ingredients. Use as a dip for chips, veggies, as a cocktail sauce or as a dressing for lettuce.

Soufflé Crackers and Triple Crème Cheese

Saltine crackers
Triple Crème cheese
Fresh whole strawberries, washed, stems on
Melted butter

Dunk saltines in ice water, quickly. Place on cookie sheet and brush with melted butter. Bake at 350° for 10 - 15 minutes. Place Triple Crème cheese in the center of a serving plate. Place berries around cheese and crackers around berries.

Strawberry Daiquiri

1 (6 oz.) can frozen daiquiri mix
1 ¼ cup light rum
2 (10 oz.) pkgs. frozen strawberries or raspberries
Finely crushed ice, about 30 cubes
6 whole strawberries, optional

Place daiquiri mix, rum and strawberries in blender. Cover and blend until smooth. Put crushed ice in large container, add daiquiri mixture, mix well and ladle into large stemmed goblets. Garnish each with a whole strawberry or use a mint leaf if raspberries were used instead of strawberries.

Serves 6.

Stuffed Pea Pods

40 sugar snap peas
1 (8 oz.) pkg. cream cheese, softened
½ lemon, juice only
1 pkg. dry Italian seasoning mix
2 cans tiny shrimp, drained

To prepare pods, remove the peas. Blanch pods for about 1 minute. In food processor, mix cream cheese, lemon juice, dry seasoning mix and 1 can of the shrimp. Fill pods with this mixture and put 1 shrimp on top of each.

Swiss Bacon Pleasers

1 (8 oz.) pkg. crescent rolls
4 slices (6 oz.) natural Swiss cheese
3 eggs, slightly beaten
¾ cup milk
1 tbsp. instant minced onion
6 - 12 slices bacon, cooked, drained and crumbled
1 tbsp. dried parsley flakes

Grease 9 x 13 x 2 pan. Separate rolls into 4 rectangles and press onto bottom and up sides of pan. Put cheese over the dough. Combine eggs, milk and onion. Pour over cheese in pan. Sprinkle with bacon and parsley. Bake at 425° 15 - 18 minutes. Cool 5 minutes and cut into 2" squares.

Makes 32 squares.

Whiskey Cup

1 ½ cups sugar
Juice of 3 lemons
2 qts. whiskey
2 qts. club soda
½ cup grenadine syrup
2 oranges, sliced
1 cup sliced pineapple

Combine sugar and lemon juice and stir. Add whiskey and soda and stir until well blended. Pour over a large block of ice in punch bowl. Add grenadine and fruit.

Serves 16.

Zippy Beef Olive Spread

1 tsp. instant minced onion
1 tbsp. dry sherry
1 (8 oz.) pkg. cream cheese
2 tbsp. mayonnaise
1 (3 oz.) pkg. chipped beef, chopped
¼ cup stuffed olives, chopped

Soften minced onion in sherry. Blend in cream cheese and mayonnaise. Stir in chipped beef and the chopped olives. This makes a terrific topper for triangles of whole wheat bread or unsalted crackers.

2 Soups

Soups can be a whole well balanced meal, a light and tasteful introduction to a dinner, main course for a luncheon or a cool, refreshing touch on a summer's day. I love to make large quantities of soup and freeze them in 1qt. plastic containers. These are apt to be hearty, thick soups. There is something delightful and comforting to sense the aroma of a kettle of simmering soup.

Beef Vegetable Soup

Delicious and hearty.

1 lb. beef stew meat, cut up
2 beef soup bones
1 onion, chopped
4 carrots, peeled and diced
4 celery ribs, chopped
1 zucchini, sliced and each slice cut in half
1 summer squash, sliced and each slice cut in half
1 (16 oz.) can cut green beans
1 (16 oz.) can corn
1 (29 oz.) can diced tomatoes
½ head green cabbage, chopped
½ box barley
3 beef bouillon cubes
V-8 juice

Brown meat and onion in large heavy sauce pan. Add rest of vegetables except cabbage. Add bouillon cubes and about 2 cups V-8 juice and 2 qts. water. Cook until vegetables are tender crisp, about 2 hours. Add cabbage and barley and cook another hour. Add more water or V-8 if needed. Remove soup bones before serving. Serve with French bread and tossed green salad.

Makes 4 qts.

Beer Cheese Soup

½ cup onion, finely chopped
¼ cup carrots, finely chopped
4 tbsp. butter
5 tbsp. flour
½ tsp. paprika
½ tsp. dry mustard
1 (12 oz.) can beer
1 cup chicken broth
1 lb. grated Cheddar cheese
1 cup heavy cream
¼ tsp. Tabasco sauce
Popcorn

Sauté onion and carrot in butter until tender. Stir in flour. Cook on low heat three to four minutes. Do not brown. Stir in paprika, mustard, beer and chicken broth. With wire whisk, stir until smooth. Add grated cheese. Let simmer 5 - 10 minutes until cheese melts. Do not boil because the cheese will curdle. Remove from heat and fold in cream. Add Tabasco and serve with popcorn as a garnish.

Serves 6.

Carrot Soup

2 lbs. carrots, peeled and chopped
1 medium potato, peeled and chopped
4 cups vegetable stock
1 cup onion, chopped
1 or 2 cloves garlic
⅓ cup almonds, finely chopped
3 tbsp. butter
½ pint heavy cream or ¾ cup sour cream

Combine carrots and potato and add to vegetable stock; bring to a boil, cover and simmer 15 minutes. Let cool to room temperature. While carrots and stock cool, sauté onion, garlic and nuts in butter until onion is transparent. Combine ingredients and purée in small amounts in blender until smooth. Reheat purée in heavy kettle or double boiler and whisk in cream. Heat slowly.

Serve with a dollop of sour cream or sprig of parsley. Cool and refrigerate for use the next day or freeze and use within a week or two.

Makes 2 qts.

Cheddar Corn Chowder

1 lb. frozen corn
4 tbsp. butter
1 lg. onion, chopped
1 green pepper, seeded and chopped
3 tbsp. flour
4 cups milk
2 cups (8 oz.) grated sharp Cheddar cheese
1 ¼ tsp. salt
¼ tsp. pepper

In large saucepan, melt butter and sauté onion and green pepper for 3 minutes. Stir in flour and continue cooking for 1 minute. Gradually stir in milk and bring almost to a boil, stirring constantly. Stir in corn and bring back almost to a boil. Reduce heat and cook 20 minutes or so. Remove from heat and cool slightly. Add cheese, salt and pepper. Can be frozen.

Makes 2 qts.

Cheesy Cream of Vegetable Soup

Terrific quick-fix vegetable soup.

2 tbsp. onion, chopped
1 tbsp. margarine or butter
1 cup frozen loose pack whole kernel corn
½ cup broccoli, chopped
¼ cup carrots, shredded
¼ cup water
1 (10 ¾ oz.) can condensed cream of potato soup
1 cup milk
¼ cup shredded Cheddar cheese
¼ cup Provolone cheese, cut up
Dash of pepper

In a medium saucepan, cook onion in butter until tender, but not brown. Add corn, broccoli, carrot and water. Bring to boil. Reduce heat. Cover and simmer 10 minutes or until vegetables are tender. Stir in soup, milk, cheeses and pepper. Cook and stir over medium heat until cheese is melted and mixture is heated through.

Serves 4 as a first course.

Chunky Sausage Chowder

3 tbsp. margarine
1 cup carrots, chopped
1 cup celery, chopped
1 green or red pepper, seeded and chopped
1 onion, chopped
4 tbsp. flour
1 tsp. salt
Pepper
1 lb. frozen corn
1 (10 oz.) Cracker Barrel Cheddar cheese, shredded
1 (1 lb.) pkg. smoked sausage
3 - 4 cups milk

Slice sausage into approx. ¼ inch thick pieces and then cut each piece into four pieces. Sauté vegetables in margarine about 20 minutes. Stir in flour. Add milk and blend. Add corn and sausage stirring often. Cook for flavors to blend about an hour. Remove from heat and add cheese. Can be frozen.

Makes 3 qts.

Clam Bisque

1 cup onion, chopped
6 tbsp. butter
6 tbsp. flour
3 (8 oz.) cans minced clams
2 (8 oz.) bottles clam juice
3 cups light cream
3 tbsp. tomato paste
3 tbsp. lemon juice

Sauté onion in butter until soft. Add flour and cook 2 minutes, stirring. Stir in clams with their liquid and the bottled clam juice. Boil 1 minute. Cover and simmer 15 minutes. Blend in blender until smooth. Add rest of ingredients, heat and serve.

Serves 12.

Cream of Artichoke Soup

½ cup shallots or green onions, chopped
1 rib celery, chopped
1 medium carrot, chopped
1 bay leaf
Pinch of thyme
½ stick butter
1 qt. chicken consommé
1 cup sliced, cooked artichoke hearts, or use canned
2 egg yolks
1 cup heavy cream
Salt and pepper

Sauté the shallots, celery, carrot, bay leaf and thyme in the butter. Add the consommé and simmer 10 to 15 minutes. Add the artichoke hearts and simmer 10 minutes. Remove from heat. Remove bay leaf. Stir the egg yolks with the cream and stir this into the soup, blending thoroughly. Season to taste with salt and pepper.

Makes about 1 ½ qts. soup.

Creamy Cheddar Cheese Soup

¼ cup margarine
½ cup onion, chopped
2 tbsp. flour
2 cups milk
2 cups canned chicken broth
2 large russet potatoes, peeled and diced
1 cup sharp Cheddar cheese
Chopped green onions or chives for garnish

Sauté onion in margarine until tender. Add flour and stir until blended. Gradually mix in milk and broth. Add potatoes. Reduce heat and simmer until potatoes are tender. Add cheese and stir until cheese is melted and smooth. Season to taste and serve with the garnish.

Serves 4.

French Soup

Easy and delicious

1 (10 ½ oz.) can cream of potato soup
1 (10 ½ oz.) can cream of chicken soup
1 (13 oz.) can chicken broth
1 pkg. chopped frozen spinach, slightly thawed

Mix all ingredients and bring just to a boil. Stir gently until spinach is thoroughly defrosted. Serve hot or chilled for a summer first course.

Serves 4.

"Hearty Soup"

Meal-in-a-bowl vegetable soup

2 ½ lbs. ground beef
2 cups onion, diced
2 ½ cups celery and leaves, diced
1 (29 oz.) can tomatoes, diced
1 (46 oz.) can V8 juice
½ cup barley
1 ½ tsp. salt
½ tsp. coarse black pepper
½ tsp. Italian seasoning
2 cups water, more as needed
2 (10 oz.) pkgs. frozen mixed vegetables

Brown the ground beef and the onion in a large soup pot. Drain and add the rest of the ingredients, except the mixed vegetables and barley. Cook for one hour. Add mixed vegetables and barley and cook an additional hour. Stir often as barley is apt to stick.

Serves 12.

Leek and Potato Soup

3 - 4 medium white potatoes (about 1 ½ lbs. total) peeled,
quartered lengthwise and sliced
1 medium onion, peeled and thinly sliced
2 large leeks or three small leeks (white parts only),
well washed, halved and thinly sliced
4 cups chicken broth, homemade if possible
1 tsp. salt
1 tsp. chervil, crumbled
½ cup heavy cream
White pepper to taste
Sour cream and chopped fresh parsley for garnish, if desired

In large soup pot or kettle, combine potatoes, onion, leeks, broth and salt; bring to a boil. Reduce heat, cover and simmer about 25 minutes or until vegetables are tender. Remove from heat and cool. Pour about 1 ½ to 2 cups of the mixture into a blender and purée until smooth. Return to soup pot. Stir in chervil and cream. Season with white pepper to taste. Return to stove and heat over medium heat, stirring often. Pour into tureen or individual cups and garnish with a dollop of sour cream sprinkled with parsley.

Serves 8.

Mother's Pea Soup

1 ham bone plus 2 cups ham, chopped
1 lb. split green peas
1 onion, chopped
1 clove garlic, crushed
3 carrots, peeled and diced
3 ribs celery, diced
1 bay leaf
½ tsp. nutmeg
½ tsp. Accent
2 qts. water
Worcestershire sauce

Combine all ingredients except the Worcestershire sauce and cook slowly for 2 - 3 hours, stirring frequently. At end of cooking time, add 1 tbsp. (or more) of Worcestershire sauce to taste and salt if needed. Remove bay leaf before serving.

Makes 3 qts.

Provençal Vegetable Soup

3 qts. water or ham stock, if possible
2 cups carrots, diced
2 cups potatoes, diced
2 cups onion, diced
1 tbsp. salt (if using water)
1 can green beans
1 can kidney beans, drained
⅓ cup broken spaghetti
1 slice stale bread, crumbled
Pinch of pepper
3 cloves garlic, crushed
4 tbsp. tomato paste
1 ½ tsp. dried basil
½ cup Parmesan cheese
¼ cup olive oil

Boil carrots, potatoes and onion in stock 40 minutes or until done. Twenty minutes before serving add green beans, kidney beans, spaghetti, bread and pepper. Boil slowly for 15 minutes. Taste for seasoning. While soup is cooking, place garlic, tomato paste, basil and cheese in a bowl or large kettle. Blend with a wooden spoon. Add olive oil slowly, beating constantly. When ready to serve, mix one cup of soup with the mixture and then add that to the remainder of the vegetables. Good served with French bread and a green salad.

Serves 8.

Wild Rice Soup

¼ cup wild rice
4 cups chicken broth
½ cup celery, diced
¼ cup onion, diced
2 tbsp. fresh mushrooms, sliced
½ cup green pepper, diced
¼ cup butter
½ cup flour
½ tsp. garlic powder
½ tsp. salt
Pepper
2 tbsp. slivered almonds
1 tbsp. pimento
1 cup half and half

Add rice to chicken broth and cook 45 minutes. Sauté celery, onion, mushrooms and green pepper in butter. Add flour and cook 2 minutes. Add garlic powder, salt, pepper, pimento and half and half to vegetables and blend. Add rice to vegetable mixture and heat through. Sprinkle almonds on top of each serving.

Serves 6.

3

Salads and Salad Dressings

Salads are favorites with many because of their cold crisp quality as accompaniments to a meal. Then, too, there are hearty salads that serve well as a main course for a luncheon. Personally, I love all kinds of salads, so read on. I hope you are inspired to try some combinations that may be new to you.

Black Cherry Jell-O Salad

This is very attractive because, when unmolded, the cheese layer is on the bottom and the Jell-O and cherries are on top. Delicious!!

1 (3 oz.) pkg. black cherry Jell-O
4 oz. cream cheese
1 can dark sweet cherries, drain and reserve juice

Soften cream cheese in microwave. Dissolve Jell-O in 1 cup boiling water. Add cheese to Jell-O mix and beat with a mixer until cheese is well blended. Add water to cherry juice to make 1 ½ cups liquid and add to Jell-O mix and blend. Stir in cherries. Do not beat. Pour into ring mold and refrigerate. When set, unmold on a plate decorated with leaf lettuce.

Serves 8-10.

Blueberry Jell-O Mold

3 (3 oz.) pkgs. lemon Jell-O
2 cans blueberries in heavy syrup, drained and syrup reserved
1 pt. sour cream
½ tsp. vanilla
1 ½ cups hot water

Dissolve 1 pkg. Jell-O in hot water. Let cool. Add sour cream and vanilla and beat until fluffy. Pour into mold and let harden well in refrigerator. Measure berry syrup and add water to make 4 cups. Heat liquid and dissolve 2 pkgs. Jell-O. When cool, add berries and pour on top of first layer. Chill.

Serves 12.

Cabbage Salad

1 pkg. broccoli slaw or 1 head cabbage, shredded
6 green onions, chopped
4 oz. sunflower seeds
1 pkg. Ramen noodle soup
2 tbsp. sugar
4 oz. slivered almonds
½ cup oil

Mix slaw or cabbage with onions. Put almonds, sunflower seeds and broken Ramen noodles on a cookie sheet and bake at 350º for 10 minutes. Watch closely. Mix oil, sugar and flavor packet from soup. When ready to serve, toss vegetables with seasonings and baked mixture. You can also keep the oil mixture and the crunchy mixture separate and mix up one or two servings with the slaw.

Serves 12.

Charlie's Potato Salad

This was served at a very fine restaurant in Minneapolis, called "Charlie's Cafe Exceptional". It was known as THE place to go.

5 medium red potatoes, peeled and freshly cooked
1 tsp. salt
Dash of white pepper
2 tbsp. green onions, chopped
2 tbsp. chopped pimento
3 hard cooked eggs, diced
1 ¼ cups mayonnaise
¼ cup celery, diced

Dice the hot potatoes (about 5 cups when diced) and sprinkle with the salt and pepper. Add remaining ingredients and mix gently. Season to taste with additional salt and pepper. Chill at least two hours.

Serves 8.

Chicken Salad

6 large chicken breasts
2 carrots, chopped
3 ribs celery, chopped
1 medium onion, sliced
1 cup celery, chopped
1 cup green seedless grapes
4 hard boiled eggs, chopped
1 can blanched almonds, browned in butter
⅓ bottle capers
12 pitted ripe olives, slivered
2 cups Hellmann's mayonnaise
2 tbsp. cream

Simmer chicken until tender with the 2 carrots, 3 ribs celery and 1 medium onion. Leave in broth overnight, refrigerated. For salad, use only the chicken. Cut in generous size pieces and add remaining salad ingredients. Blend mayonnaise with cream. Mix all together lightly and serve on lettuce. Also delicious served in cantaloupe ring.

Serves 8.

Colonial Inn Dressing

8 tbsp. sugar, or more
1 tbsp. prepared mustard
1 tbsp. salt
Paprika
1 tbsp. Worcestershire sauce
½ cup vinegar
¾ cup oil
1 can tomato soup, undiluted
1 small onion, minced

Combine well. Good on fruit salad or mixed greens.

Egg Ring Salad

2 tbsp. gelatin
1 ½ cups cold water
12 eggs, hard boiled
1 pt. mayonnaise
½ cup catsup
2 tbsp. lemon juice
2 tbsp. Worcestershire
2 tbsp. fresh parsley, chopped
½ tbsp. minced onion
1 lb. crabmeat or chicken or shrimp
Garnish, if desired, with artichoke hearts, tomato wedges and olives

Continued on next page

Sauce

1 cup catsup
¼ tsp. salt
2 drops Tabasco
2 tbsp. lemon juice
1 cup cream, whipped

For Salad
In a small bowl, soak gelatin in cold water for 5 minutes. Set bowl over small amount of hot water and stir until dissolved. Add lemon juice, Worcestershire, parsley, onion and catsup. Chill and let partially set. Add mayonnaise and chopped eggs. Pour into well oiled ring mold and chill. When ready to serve, unmold on a large platter lined with curly endive. Fill center with 1 lb. crabmeat, chicken or shrimp. Garnish with artichoke hearts, tomato wedges and olives

For Sauce
Mix all but cream and add whipped cream at the very last just before pouring over the molded salad.

This will easily serve 12. The egg mixture fills an additional small mold besides the ring. Serve with hot sour dough French rolls. For dessert, lemon sherbet with Crème de Menthe.

Fresh Fruit Salad

4 medium apples, unpeeled and diced
4 bananas, sliced
Juice of one lemon
1 pineapple, cubed
1 cup fresh berries
1 cup cream sherry
Mint sprigs

Combine apples and bananas in bowl and sprinkle with lemon juice. Add rest of ingredients except mint. Mix well and refrigerate 1 - 2 hours. Toss again before serving and garnish with mint.

Serves 8.

Frozen Pineapple Cranberry Salad

1 can (16oz) crushed pineapple
1 can whole cranberry sauce
1 cup sour cream
¼ cup pecans, coarsely chopped

Combine all ingredients and spoon into an 8" square pan. Freeze. Cut in squares and arrange on crisp greens. Great served with turkey or chicken.

Serves 8.

Gazpacho Relish Salad

⅓ cup Italian dressing or vinegar and oil
¼ cup tomato sauce
4 green onions, chopped
1 medium green pepper, cut in strips
1 cucumber, sliced
2 tomatoes, cut in wedges
1 cup celery, sliced diagonally
Tabasco

In small bowl blend dressing, tomato sauce, green onions and dash of Tabasco. Layer green pepper, cucumber, tomato and celery adding dressing between each layer. Chill 4 hours or overnight.
Stir occasionally.

Serves 4 - 6.

Herbed Tomatoes

4 large, ripe tomatoes
6 tbsp. fresh parsley, chopped
2 cloves garlic, crushed
¾ cup olive oil
3 tbsp. wine vinegar
1 tsp. salt
½ tsp. dried leaf basil
⅓ tsp. pepper
Dash of Fines Herbs
¼ tsp. dill weed

Cut tomatoes into medium slices. Place in a container with tight lid. Mix all seasonings together with the oil and pour over tomatoes. Chill 2 - 3 hours.

Really good served with grilled steak, corn on the cob and garlic toast.

Honey Dressing - for fruit

1 cup sugar
1 cup oil
½ cup vinegar
¾ tsp. dry mustard
¾ tsp. paprika
½ tsp. salt
Few drops lemon juice
Small amount of grated onion
1 tsp. celery seed

Combine and beat 15 minutes. Delicious!

Hot Bacon Dressing Salad

Delicious!

5 slices bacon, diced and fried, reserve fat
Bowl of cut up red leaf lettuce
2 hard boiled eggs, sliced
3 green onions, chopped
½ tsp. salt
½ tsp. dry mustard
2 tsp. sugar
1 tsp. flour
½ cup vinegar
¼ cup water

Fry the bacon, remove from pan and drain on paper towel. Crumble over lettuce and add eggs and green onions. To bacon fat, add rest of ingredients and cook until blended and bubbly. Pour, very hot, over salad just before serving.

Serves 4.

Hot Baked Potato Salad

This is good with steak, ham or brats.
Any leftovers are good cold the next day.

8 red skinned potatoes (about 2 lbs.)
6 slices bacon, diced and fried until brown
¾ cup green onions (including tops), chopped
¾ cup green pepper, chopped
¾ cup celery, chopped
1 cup sour cream
⅓ cup mayonnaise
⅓ cup white wine vinegar
2 tbsp. Dijon mustard
1 tbsp. sugar
1 tsp. celery seed
1 tsp. salt
2 tbsp. bacon drippings
2 hard cooked eggs, sliced
Chopped parsley

Boil potatoes until tender. While still very warm, peel and cut into chunks. Mix with the bacon, green onions, green pepper and celery. In a small bowl, mix the sour cream, mayonnaise, vinegar, mustard, sugar, celery seed, salt and bacon drippings. Add to the warm potato mixture and mix well. Put in a casserole and heat at 325° for about 30 minutes or until bubbly. Garnish with eggs and parsley.

Serves 6.

Italian Pasta Salad

4 cups (16 oz.) rotini pasta, uncooked
1 (12 oz.) jar marinated artichoke hearts
1 (16 oz.) can mushrooms
2 cups celery, sliced diagonally
1 cup green pepper, chopped
8 oz. mozzarella, cut in ½" cubes
8 oz. Cotto salami, cut julienne
1 medium red onion, sliced thinly
2 cups ripe olives, sliced

Marinade
¼ cup oil
2 tbsp. white wine vinegar
1 tsp. dry mustard
¼ tsp. dry oregano
¾ tsp. dried basil
½ tsp. salt
½ to 1 tsp. minced garlic
¼ cup Parmesan cheese.

For Salad
Cook pasta according to package directions. Drain and run cold water over it. Drain well. Make marinade by mixing all ingredients together except the Parmesan cheese. Add marinade and rest of ingredients to the pasta. Marinate overnight. Before serving, add Parmesan cheese.

Serves 8.

Lou's Salad

Spinach, Bibb lettuce, Boston lettuce, romaine
3 hard boiled eggs, peeled and sliced in sixths
8 slices bacon, fried and crumbled
Red onion slices
½ cup mayonnaise
¼ cup cider vinegar
½ cup sugar

Put greens in salad bowl and add eggs, bacon and red onion. Make dressing by mixing the mayonnaise, vinegar and sugar. Dress salad just before serving.

Luncheon Salad

2 lbs. cooked chicken or turkey, diced
2 lbs. cooked ham, diced
2 lbs. grated Cheddar cheese
2 lbs. bacon, fried and crumbled
1 dozen eggs, hard cooked and chopped
3 to 4 ripe avocados, diced
1 lb. fresh mushrooms, sliced
1 (7 ¾ oz.) can pitted ripe olives, sliced
2 bunches green onions, sliced
1 ½ pts. cherry tomatoes, halved
3 (6 oz.) jars marinated artichoke hearts, diced
5 - 6 heads lettuce, preferably mixed greens

Dressing
1 cup oil
⅓ cup wine vinegar
½ tsp. dry mustard
½ tsp. garlic powder
1 tsp. sugar
½ tsp. salad herbs
Salt and pepper and reserved artichoke juice

Marinate the mushrooms and artichoke hearts in dressing 3 - 4 hours. Mix all remaining ingredients in very large bowl, add marinated mushrooms and artichoke hearts, and toss.

Serve with Sangria, warm muffins and brownies.

Serves 24.

Make Ahead Chef Salad

6 cups shredded lettuce (iceberg, romaine or a combination)
3 medium carrots, shredded
4 green onions (including tops), thinly sliced
3 stalks celery, sliced
3 cups cooked chicken or turkey, shredded
1 (2 ¼ oz.) can sliced ripe olives, drained
1 ½ cups mayonnaise
1 tbsp. Dijon mustard
2 tbsp. mild red onion, minced
1 clove garlic, minced or pressed
¼ tsp. Italian herbs
¼ tsp. paprika
Salt and pepper
2 medium-sized tomatoes
2 hard cooked eggs
6 slices bacon, crisply cooked and crumbled
2 tbsp. parsley, chopped

Arrange lettuce in an even layer in a shallow 4 qt. serving dish. (a 9 x 13 inch baking dish works fine). Top with carrots, green onions, celery, chicken and olives. In a small bowl, stir together mayonnaise, mustard, red onion, garlic, herb seasoning and paprika. Season to taste with salt and pepper. Spread dressing evenly over chicken mixture. Cover and refrigerate at least 2 hours or until the next day. Just before serving, cut tomatoes into wedges and slice eggs; decoratively arrange atop salad. Sprinkle with bacon and parsley. For each serving, scoop down to bottom of dish and lift out a portion of all layers.

Makes about 6 servings.

Mandarin Chicken Salad

One and one half recipe will serve 16 ladies for lunch.

2 cups cooked chicken, chopped
1 tbsp. green onion, sliced
1 tsp. salt
1 cup grapes
1 can pineapple chunks, drained
1 cup celery, chopped
1 cup mandarin oranges, drained
½ cup almonds, sliced
1 cup macaroni rings, cooked
1 cup mayonnaise
1 cup cream, whipped

Combine chicken, onion, celery, salt and mayonnaise and macaroni rings. Refrigerate. When ready to serve, add the well drained fruit, sliced almonds and lastly the whipped cream.

Serves 10.

Molded Shrimp Salad

1 can tomato soup
1 (8 oz.) pkg. cream cheese, softened
2 tbsp. gelatin (1 envelope=1tbsp, use two envelopes)
½ cup cold water
1 cup mayonnaise
2 cups shrimp or 3 (4 ½ oz.) cans shrimp
1 ½ cups celery, chopped
1 small onion, grated
¼ cup green pepper, chopped

Start to heat soup. Dissolve gelatin in water and add to soup as it heats. Stir with whisk and add cream cheese. Do not boil. When cheese is melted, remove from heat. Let cool 30 minutes and then add the rest of the ingredients. Mix well and pour into a salad mold and chill at least 4 - 5 hours.

Serve with deviled eggs and tomato wedges.

Serves 6 - 8.

Mother's Oil/Vinegar Dressing

This is a favorite-everyone raves about it when it's served.

⅔ cup oil
⅓ cup red wine vinegar
1 tbsp. salt
1 tsp. paprika
1 tsp. ground mustard
1 tsp. salad herbs
1 tsp. parsley flakes

Combine all ingredients and mix well. A clean covered jar works well.

Makes 1 cup.

Mother's Potato Salad

6 medium red new potatoes, unpeeled
½ cup sour cream
½ cup mayonnaise
6 green onions, chopped
4 tbsp. diced pimento

Scrub potatoes. In saucepan, cook potatoes in 1" boiling water with 1 tsp. salt until barely tender—about 20 minutes. Drain potatoes. Peel and cut into cubes. In large bowl, make a layer of potatoes, add a little salt, some green onion and pimento. Repeat layers until all ingredients are used. Then add sour cream and mayonnaise. Mix well and chill.

Serves 6 - 8

Orange Salad

2 (3 oz.) pkgs. orange Jell-O
2 cups hot water
1 pt. orange sherbet
½ pt. whipped cream
1 large can mandarin oranges, drained

Mix Jell-O and water and let partially cool but not set. Fold in sherbet, whipped cream and oranges. Makes a big ring mold or 2 smaller molds. Chill.

Orange Salad Dressing for Spinach Salad

¼ cup light olive oil
⅓ cup rice wine vinegar
3 tbsp. frozen orange juice concentrate
2 tbsp. honey
Salt to taste
Hot red pepper sauce—drops to taste

Use on baby spinach with a combination of dried cranberries, orange slices, walnuts.

Oriental Chicken Salad

4 tbsp. slivered almonds
2 tbsp. sesame seeds
1 head romaine, shredded
4 cups chow mein noodles
3 cups cooked chicken, cut in strips
3 green onions, cut long and into thirds

Dressing
4 tbsp. sugar
2 tsp. salt
1 tsp. pepper
½ cup salad oil
6 tbsp. vinegar (rice or wine)

Toast almonds and sesame seeds separately in a dry skillet over medium heat. Stir until toasted. Arrange lettuce, chicken, onions, chow mein noodles, almonds and sesame seeds in large salad bowl. Dress and toss.

Serve with small orange rolls, potato chips and stuffed olives.

Serves 8 - 10

Overnight Pasta Salad

1 cup tiny shell macaroni
1 cup cooked ham, julienne
2 cups lettuce, shredded
2 hard boiled eggs, sliced
1 cup frozen peas
½ cup or more, Swiss cheese, shredded or julienne
Garnish, if desired, with paprika and snipped parsley.

Dressing
½ cup mayonnaise
¼ cup sour cream
1 tbsp. green onion, chopped
1 tsp. prepared mustard
Few drops Tabasco

Cook shells, rinse, drain and cool. Place lettuce in bottom of a 2 qt. casserole, sprinkle with salt and pepper. Top with the shells, then egg slices, ham strips, peas and lastly the cheese. Combine all ingredients for the dressing and spread over top of the salad sealing to the edge. Cover and refrigerate 24 hours or overnight. Sprinkle with paprika and snipped parsley. Toss before serving.

Serves 4-6.

Pea-Nut Salad

2 (10 oz.) pkgs. frozen peas, thawed and drained but not cooked
1 cup celery, chopped
½ cup onion, chopped
2 to 2 ½ cups sour cream
1 tsp. Worcestershire sauce
1 tsp. garlic salt
1 tsp. lemon juice
1 ½ cup cashews, coarsely chopped
¼ lb. bacon, cooked until crisp and well drained
Hollow tomato cups or lettuce leaves, if desired, for serving

In large bowl, combine peas, celery and onion. Stir in sour cream. Sprinkle with Worcestershire, garlic salt, lemon juice and cashews. Crumble bacon over mixture and stir until just mixed. Store in covered container in refrigerator overnight.
Serve in hollowed tomato cups or on greens.

Serves 6 - 8.

Shrimp Salad

1 long loaf sandwich bread, crusts removed and cut into 16 pieces per slice
¾ qt. Hellmann's mayonnaise
4 hard cooked eggs, diced
1 large onion, diced
3 cans small shrimp

Mix together and let sit overnight.

Serves 10.

Spanish Salad

Fresh asparagus, blanched and chilled
Cherry tomatoes, halved
Green olives, sliced
Red pepper, cut in strips
Artichoke hearts, quartered
Boston or leaf lettuce

Dressing
⅓ cup olive oil
⅓ cup wine vinegar
2 tbsp. green onions, sliced
½ tsp. salt

Use a large glass plate and line with lettuce. Put asparagus across center. Arrange cherry tomatoes in 4 places (north, south, east and west). Put olives and artichoke in between tomatoes. Lay red pepper strips on top of asparagus. Pour dressing over all. Very pretty.

Summer Salad

2 - 3 cups cut up greens
2 cups cooked chicken, diced
1 cucumber, diced
2 ripe tomatoes, chopped
½ green pepper, diced
1 onion, chopped
½ lb. bacon, cooked and crumbled
1 avocado, sliced
Roasted diced almonds or sautéed walnuts
Tomato wedges and cucumber slices for garnish

Dressing
1 cup mayonnaise
1 cup sour cream
¼ cup wine vinegar
1 tsp. Italian herbs
⅛ tsp. garlic powder
3 tbsp. grated Parmesan cheese

Combine dressing ingredients. Cover and chill for at least 1 hour. Makes about 2 ¼ cups

For Salad
Layer the greens and chicken in a salad bowl. Combine cucumber, tomato, green pepper and onion with a little of the dressing and let marinate in refrigerator for an hour. Spread over chicken. Sprinkle bacon on for next layer. Top with avocado and lastly the nuts. Garnish with some tomato wedges and cucumber slices, add dressing and toss.
Serves 6.

Superb Tossed Salad

1 head romaine
1 head Bibb lettuce
1 small head iceberg lettuce
½ cup shredded Parmesan cheese
½ cup (2 oz.) blue cheese, crumbled
3 avocados
1 ½ cups cucumber, peeled and sliced (about 1 large)
1 ½ cups cherry tomatoes, halved
6 slices bacon, crisp-cooked, drained and crumbled
Red and green pepper slices
½ cup ripe olives, sliced
Italian salad dressing

Tear salad greens into bite size pieces; combine in large salad bowl. Sprinkle the cheeses over greens. Halve avocados; remove seeds and peel. Slice crosswise with fluted vegetable cutter. Arrange avocado slices, cucumber, tomatoes, bacon, pepper slices and olives atop salad. To serve, pour Italian dressing over all and toss.

Serves 12.

Sweet French Dressing

¾ cup catsup
⅓ cup sugar
¼ cup vinegar
½ cup salad oil
Salt
Pepper
Onion salt

Put all in a pint jar and shake well to mix.

Sweet Oil Dressing

1 tsp. salt
½ tsp. Tabasco
4 tbsp. sugar
4 tbsp. tarragon vinegar
½ cup salad oil
Dash of pepper

Mix well and refrigerate.

Thousand Island Dressing

1 pt. mayonnaise
1 bottle Heinz chili sauce
1 tbsp. vinegar
1 tbsp. sugar
3 hard cooked eggs, diced

Mix all together carefully. Serve on mixed salad greens.

Makes 4 cups.

Vegetable Bouquet Salad

1 can cut green beans, drained
1 can red kidney beans, drained
1 (7 oz.) can pitted ripe olives, drained
1 (15 oz.) can artichoke hearts, drained
1 ½ cups celery, diagonally sliced
1 medium onion, thinly sliced
1 (4 oz.) jar pimento, drained
1 can whole mushrooms, drained
2 tbsp. capers
1 ½ tsp. salt
1 tsp. sugar
*1 tbsp. herbs
¼ tsp. Tabasco
½ cup salad oil
¼ cup tarragon vinegar
¼ cup fresh parsley, chopped
1 ½ tsp. MSG, optional

Combine drained vegetables, celery and onion. Measure vinegar, MSG, salt and sugar and stir until dissolved. *Add herbs (use your own judgment and pick from the following: Summer Savory, Fines Herbs, garlic powder, dill weed, Beau Monde, Italian seasoning-or use a little of all of them.) Add Tabasco and salad oil. Beat or shake until well blended. Pour over vegetables and refrigerate. Turn into serving bowl and sprinkle with parsley and capers.

Egg Dishes

Eggs are nourishing and so versatile.
Whether as a main course for a brunch
or as deviled eggs for a picnic,
they always are good. Hard-boiled eggs
compliment salads and soft-boiled eggs
are good for breakfast. You can be creative
with eggs and make omelets or soufflés
as well as many other dishes.

Bacon and Egg Strata

8 slices bacon, fried crisp, drained and crumbled
2 tbsp. margarine
½ cup dried bread crumbs
2 cups soft bread crumbs, about 4 slices of bread
1 ¾ cups milk
8 eggs
Salt and pepper
Lawry's salt
4 tbsp. butter
½ lb. sliced Swiss cheese

Melt margarine in small pan. Add dried bread crumbs and bacon. Set aside. Soak soft bread crumbs in milk. Drain, reserving milk. Combine milk with eggs and whisk. Add salt and pepper. Melt butter in a heavy skillet and cook eggs until soft, but not fully cooked. Add soft bread crumbs to eggs and turn into a greased 9 x 9 pan. Sprinkle with Lawry's salt. Put on Swiss cheese slices. Sprinkle with bacon mixture. Bake at 400° for 20 - 25 minutes. Cover for first 10 minutes.

Serves 6 - 8.

Breakfast Casserole

2 tbsp. butter
2 cups (8 oz.) shredded Swiss or sharp Cheddar cheese
12 eggs
Salt and pepper
1 (12-16 oz.) roll ground sausage, sliced into 15 pieces and fried
1 (4 oz.) can mushroom pieces, drained
⅔ cup half and half
Paprika
Parsley flakes

Spread butter in a 9 x 13 baking pan. Sprinkle half the cheese over butter. Break eggs on top of cheese and poke yolks, but do not stir. Sprinkle salt and pepper to taste. Top with cooked sausage and add mushrooms. Pour half and half over and top with rest of cheese. Add paprika and parsley to taste. Bake at 350° for 30 minutes. Let stand 5 minutes and cut into pieces.

Serves 12 - 15.

Crab Supper Quiche

9 inch pie shell, unbaked
1 cup (4 oz.) Swiss cheese, shredded
1 (7 ½ oz.) can crab
2 green onions, sliced
3 eggs, beaten
1 cup half and half
½ tsp. salt
½ tsp. lemon peel, grated
¼ tsp. dry mustard
Dash of mace
¼ cup sliced almonds

Sprinkle cheese on pie shell then add crab and onions. Combine eggs, cream and seasonings and pour over. Top with almonds. Bake at 325º for 45 minutes.

Serves 4 - 6.

Custom Omelet

8 slices uncooked bacon, diced
½ green pepper, diced
1 bunch green onions, chopped
4 oz. cooked ham, diced
½ cup canned artichoke hearts, drained and diced
¼ cup black olives, sliced
8 eggs
½ can beer at room temperature
Salt and pepper
1 ½ cups sharp Cheddar cheese, grated
Sliced tomatoes
Parsley

Sauté bacon until almost done. Add green pepper and onion and sauté. Drain fat. Using a separate, oven-proof skillet, melt 1 tbsp. margarine in pan. Add bacon mix. Sprinkle ham, artichoke hearts and olives over. Beat eggs with beer and add salt and pepper. Pour into skillet and sprinkle with cheese. Bake until center is firm, about 25 minutes. Cut in wedges and garnish. Start oven at 450° and immediately turn to 350° when you put pan in.

Serves 6-8.

Easy Oven-Baked French Toast

16 slices white sandwich bread, cut into 1 inch cubes
1 (8 oz.) pkg. cream cheese, softened
12 large eggs
2 cups whipping cream
½ cup maple syrup
½ tsp. maple flavoring
Maple syrup

Place bread cubes in a lightly greased 13 x 9 x 2 inch baking dish; set aside. Beat cream cheese at medium speed with an electric mixer until smooth. Add eggs and next three ingredients, beating until blended. Pour over bread cubes; cover and refrigerate 8 hours or over night. Remove from refrigerator; let stand at room temperature 30 minutes. Bake at 375° for 40 to 50 minutes until set, covering with foil after 25 minutes. Serve with additional syrup.

Serves 15.

Egg Soufflé

8 slices bread, buttered and cubed, divided
1 ½ cup grated Swiss or Cheddar cheese, divided
2 cans (4 oz. each) sliced mushrooms OR ½ lb. sliced fresh
mushrooms,sautéed in 2 tbsp. butter
4 - 6 oz. cubed cooked ham
4 small green onions (including green tops), thinly sliced
1 small jar chopped pimento
5 eggs beaten
2 ½ cups milk
¾ tsp. salt
¾ tsp. dry mustard

Place half of the bread cubes in a 9 x 13 baking dish and sprinkle with half of the grated cheese. Layer mushrooms over cheese, then ham, onions and pimento. Cover with remaining bread cubes. In medium bowl, combine beaten eggs, milk, salt and dry mustard. Beat until well mixed and pour over contents of casserole. Sprinkle with remaining cheese. Bake at 350º 45 - 60 minutes, until top is lightly browned. Let stand 10 minutes before cutting into squares to serve.

Serves 10.

Eggs à la Suisse

1 tbsp. butter
½ cup cream
4 eggs
Salt and pepper
Dash of cayenne
Grated Cheddar cheese
Whole wheat toast, buttered
Sherry-optional

Melt butter in skillet and add cream. Break in eggs one at a time. Sprinkle with salt and pepper and cayenne. Cook gently until whites are nearly firm. Sprinkle with grated cheese and cook to desired consistency. Serve over buttered toast with cream from pan poured over. Sherry can be added to cream, if desired, before pouring. Excellent for Sunday breakfast, brunch or luncheon dish.

Serves 4.

Eggs and Sausage Casserole

6 slices white bread
1 lb. sausage meat
1 tsp. prepared mustard
1 cup shredded Swiss cheese
3 eggs, slightly beaten
1 cup milk
¾ cup light cream
¼ tsp. salt
Freshly ground pepper
Dash nutmeg
1 tsp. Worcestershire sauce

Place bread in a well buttered 9 x 13 casserole to cover bottom. Cook sausage in skillet until done. Drain off fat. Mix with mustard. Sprinkle sausage evenly over bread, then sprinkle cheese over sausage. Combine eggs, milk, cream and seasonings and pour over casserole. Bake at 350º for 30 - 35 minutes, or until set.

Serves 6.

Fancy Egg Scramble-Yummy!

Serve with fresh fruit compote and muffins

1 cup (4 oz.) Canadian bacon, diced
¼ cup green onions, chopped
3 tbsp. margarine
12 eggs, beaten
½ lb. fresh mushrooms
4 tsp. (or more) butter, melted
2 ½ cups soft bread crumbs (3 slices)
⅛ tsp. paprika
1 recipe cheese sauce.

Sauce
2 tbsp. butter or margarine
2 tbsp. flour
½ tsp. salt
½ tsp. pepper
2 cups milk
1 cup (or more) sharp Cheddar cheese, grated

For Sauce
Melt 2 tbsp. butter or margarine. Blend in 2 tbsp. flour, ½ tsp. salt and pepper. Add 2 cups milk. Stir in 1 cup (or more) of sharp Cheddar cheese.

For Eggs
In skillet, sauté bacon, onion and sliced mushrooms in 3 tbsp. margarine until onion is tender but not brown. In another skillet, scramble eggs until just set. Add cheese sauce and bacon mixture to eggs. Add bread crumbs mixed with butter and paprika to eggs. Turn into a 12 x 7 x 2 baking dish. Cover and chill until 30 minutes before serving. Bake uncovered at 350º for 30 minutes.

Serves 10.

Farmer's Omelet

3 tbsp. butter or margarine
2 cups cold boiled potatoes, cubed
⅓ cup onion, finely chopped
½ cup green pepper, finely chopped
1 clove garlic, minced
1 cup ham, cubed
¼ cup fresh parsley, chopped
6 eggs
1 tsp. salt
⅛ tsp. fresh ground pepper
2 tbsp. milk
1 cup shredded Monterey Jack cheese

In 9 inch skillet, melt butter. Add potatoes, onion, green pepper and garlic. Cook over medium heat, stirring occasionally, until lightly browned, about 5 minutes. Add ham and cook until heated throughout; sprinkle with parsley and reduce heat. In medium bowl, beat eggs, salt, pepper and milk until well blended. Pour egg mixture over potato mixture; cover and cook until eggs are almost set, about 10 minutes, slipping spatula around edges of pan occasionally to allow eggs to run down. Sprinkle with cheese, cover and cook until cheese melts. Cut into wedges to serve.

Serves 4-6.

Savory Eggs

1 cup Cheddar cheese, grated
1 tbsp. margarine
½ cup milk
1 tsp. prepared mustard
½ tsp. salt
¼ tsp. pepper
6 eggs, slightly beaten

Heat oven to 325°. Sprinkle cheese in a 9 inch square pan and dot with margarine. Mix milk, mustard and salt and pepper. Pour half over cheese. Pour eggs on top, then remaining milk mixture. Bake uncovered for 25 minutes.

Serve with grapefruit and orange fruit bowl, sweet rolls and sausage.

Serves 6.

Scrambled Eggs for a Crowd

18 eggs
1 cup + 2 tbsp. half and half
2 - 3 tbsp. butter
1 can cream of mushroom soup
2 cans (4 oz.) mushroom pieces
2 cups shredded Cheddar cheese
1 (2 oz.) jar pimento
2 - 3 tbsp. green onions, sliced

Beat eggs with half and half; scramble in hot butter.
Put eggs in a 13 x 9 shallow baking dish. Combine remaining ingredients and spread over eggs. Bake in preheated oven at 250º for 45 - 60 minutes. Cooked casserole will hold in oven up to 45 minutes. To prepare ahead: Cover and refrigerate. Bake for 1 ½ hours.

Serves 10 -12.

5

Fish and Sea Food

For many people eating light now means eating fish. Use fresh fish if you possibly can. Whole fish are more perishable so they are usually fresher than fillets. Most fish are seasonal so we need to learn to substitute within fish types. If you are tired of Tuna or Salmon, this chapter offers some interesting options.

Baked Fish Fillets

Fish Fillets
Accent
Lemon juice
Salt
Equal amounts of mayonnaise and sour cream
Paprika

Lay fish on a flat, greased pan. Season with Accent, lemon juice and salt. Blend mayonnaise and sour cream and cover fish with the sauce. Sprinkle with paprika. Bake at 375° for about 20 minutes.

Serve with parsley buttered new potatoes, broccoli spears or fresh asparagus and a salad of sliced tomatoes, cucumbers and onion rings marinated in tart vinegar and oil dressing.

Basic Butter Sauce

¼ cup butter, melted
4 tbsp. lemon juice
2 tbsp. Worcestershire
Dash of Tabasco

Blend all ingredients. Put fish fillets on foil on cookie sheet. Pour sauce over fish, enough to baste with while baking. Bake 30 minutes at 350°.

Creamed Scallops and Mushrooms

½ lb. scallops
½ lb. mushrooms
½ cup dry white wine
4 tbsp. margarine, divided
2 tbsp. flour
1 cup milk

Wash the scallops and drain on paper towels. Put into saucepan with the wine. Bring to a boil and simmer for 5 minutes. Drain off the liquid and reserve. Set aside the scallops. Clean and slice the mushrooms. Sauté for 5 minutes in 2 tbsp. margarine. Set aside.
In a fry pan, heat 2 tbsp. margarine, add flour and blend and cook for a few minutes. Add milk and the reserved scallop liquid. Cook a few minutes, then add the mushrooms and scallops and heat through gently.

Serve with whole green beans and a fresh vegetable salad dressed with Green Goddess dressing.

Serves 4.

Fish Vegetable Sauté

12 oz. fresh fish fillets, pollock or halibut, cut into 1" chunks.
1 cup sliced mushrooms
1 cup broccoli florets
1 medium onion, halved and thinly sliced
3 tbsp. oil
1 medium firm ripe tomato, diced
3 tbsp. water
1 tbsp. cornstarch
Dash of ground pepper
Dash of thyme

Sauté mushrooms, broccoli and onion in 2 tbsp. oil in wok until tender crisp. Set aside. Sauté fish about 2 minutes in rest of oil; add tomato and heat. Return vegetables to pan. Combine cornstarch and water and add to pan. Add ground pepper and thyme. Cook 1 minute longer until fish flakes easily.

Serves 3.

Halibut Bake

4 halibut steaks
Salt and pepper
1 cup sour cream
¼ cup onion, chopped
2 tbsp. parsley
2 tbsp. pimento, chopped
¼ cup Parmesan, grated
1 tsp. Worcestershire
Paprika

Heat oven to 375º. Place fish in well buttered 10 x 6 x 2 baking pan; add salt and pepper. Bake for 25 minutes. Combine next 4 ingredients and spread over fish. Sprinkle top with cheese, Worcestershire and paprika. Bake 5 - 7 minutes longer.

Serves 4.

Hot Seafood Salad

3 (7 ½ oz.) cans crabmeat
1 ½ lbs. de-veined and shelled frozen shrimp
4 cups mayonnaise
4 cups celery, diced
2 green peppers, diced
1 medium onion, diced
8 hard cooked eggs, chopped
4 tsp. Worcestershire
2 tsp. salt
2 (8 oz.) cans sliced water chestnuts
8 oz. slivered almonds
Dry bread crumbs

Mix all ingredients except almonds and bread crumbs and put in a casserole the night before. Press down dry bread crumbs on top and sprinkle with almonds. Bake 30 minutes at 350°.

Serves 20.

Salmon Loaf

1 (1 lb.) can red salmon
1 ½ cups milk
1 ½ slices bread or 8 Waverly crackers
2 to 4 tbsp. margarine
2 or 3 eggs
½ tsp. salt

Skin, bone and flake salmon. Should equal 2 cups. Combine milk, bread or crackers, margarine and salt and heat (not boil). Beat eggs quite well, add to salmon and then to rest of ingredients. Bake for 1 hour at 350º in an 8" square pan or a loaf pan 8¼ x 4½ x 3. Best prepared ahead of time.

Serves 6 - 8.

Seafood Hot Dish

1 ¼ cups celery, chopped
1 medium onion, chopped
1 medium green pepper, chopped
1 (10 oz.) pkg. frozen peas
¾ lb. mock crab legs, cut up
1 bag frozen peeled, de-veined shrimp, thawed
½ lb. mushrooms
1 tbsp. Worcestershire sauce
1 ⅛ cups mayonnaise
1 (8 oz.) can sliced water chestnuts

In a small amount of oil, sauté celery, onion, green pepper and mushrooms. Mix Worcestershire sauce with mayonnaise and add to sautéed vegetables. Add remaining ingredients and bake at 350° for about 45 minutes. Can be prepared the day before and brought to room temperature before baking.

Serves 10.

Shrimp Curry

2 tbsp. oil
½ cup celery, chopped
½ cup onion, chopped
1 clove garlic, minced
2 tbsp. flour
1 cup milk
¾ cup water
½ cup applesauce
2 scant tbsp. tomato paste
3 tsp. curry powder, or more to taste
2 tsp. chicken bouillon
Salt, garlic powder and Accent to taste
1 (16 oz.) bag frozen, cooked and shelled shrimp, thawed
2 (4 oz.) cans tiny shrimp, drained
2 generous tbsp. sour cream
Hot cooked rice
Major Greys Chutney
Green onions, chopped
Salted peanuts

Sauté celery, onion and garlic in the oil. Blend in flour. Stir in milk, water, applesauce, tomato paste, curry and bouillon. Add other seasonings to taste. Cook and stir until thickened and bubbly. Add shrimp and cook on low heat 10 minutes. Reduce heat and add sour cream. Mix and serve over hot cooked rice. Serve with Major Grey's Chutney, chopped green onions and salted peanuts.

Serves 6 - 8.

Shrimp and Scallops Gruyère

1 lb. scallops
1 lb. cooked shrimp
¾ cup + 2 tbsp. butter or margarine
¾ cup flour
3 cups milk
12 oz. Swiss Gruyère cheese,cut in small pieces
¼ tsp. garlic powder
3 ½ tsp. salt
¼ tsp. white pepper
¼ tsp. Accent
¼ tsp. dry mustard
2 tsp. tomato paste
3 tsp. lemon juice
½ lb. mushrooms, sliced
2 tbsp. green pepper, diced

Make a cream sauce in the top of a double boiler with ¾ cup butter, the flour and milk. Add cheese and stir until melted. Add seasonings. Poach scallops for 10 minutes in water to which you have added ½ tsp. salt and 1 tsp. lemon juice. Set aside and reserve broth. Add ½ cup of broth to cream sauce. Sauté mushrooms in 2 tbsp. butter and add to sauce. Drain scallops and add with the shrimp to the sauce. Heat for 10 - 15 minutes. Garnish top with the green pepper that has been sautéed in butter until tender. Serve with rice.

Serves 8.

Main Dishes

Deciding what to serve as an entrée usually takes the most time and thought. Whether you choose Barbecued Country Ribs, Chicken in Phyllo, or Priscilla's Macaroni and Cheese, you will find a lot of choices in this chapter. Usually you will make a decision for your main course and then plan other dishes to compliment each other as well as the entrées. In some of the recipes that follow, Mother included several serving suggestions.

All in One Chicken Dinner

4 onions, sliced
4 potatoes, sliced
4 chicken thighs and legs, or 4 chicken breasts
2 cups fresh broccoli florets
4 tbsp. butter
4 tbsp. flour
2 cups half and half
½ lb. Cheddar cheese, grated

In baking dish, layer potatoes and onions then top with chicken. Make cream sauce with the butter, flour and half and half. Add cheese and blend in cream sauce. Cover chicken with cheese sauce and bake at 350º for 45 minutes. Then add the broccoli (which has been blanched for 5 minutes) around the edges and bake for 15 minutes more.

Serve with Hot Curried Fruit.

Serves 4.

Barbecue Hamburgers

¾ lb. hamburger
¼ cup bread crumbs
¾ tsp. salt
¼ cup milk
½ cup ketchup
1 tbsp. sugar
1 ½ tbsp. vinegar
¼ tsp. dry mustard
½ tsp. Worcestershire
Salt to taste

Make first 4 ingredients into patties and brown. Combine rest to make sauce. Pour over patties and refrigerate for a day. Bring to room temperature and heat at 350° for 30 minutes or until thoroughly heated. Serve with buns.

Serves 3 - 4.

Barbecued Country Spareribs

1 recipe of Country Barbecue Sauce *(see next page)*
4 - 5 lbs. country spareribs, cut into 1 or 2 inch pieces
2 cups water
½ cup soy sauce
1 tbsp. freshly ground pepper
1 tsp. dried marjoram

Prepare barbecue sauce and let stand overnight or several hours. Put spareribs in large saucepan and add water, soy sauce, pepper and marjoram. Bring to boil and let simmer about half an hour, turning ribs in liquid so they cook evenly. Drain ribs and discard liquid. Combine ribs with barbecue sauce and bring to a boil. Let stand until ready to cook. Ribs may be prepared to this point several hours in advance. Preheat oven to 350° or prepare charcoal fire for grilling. Reheat ribs in sauce. Spoon and scrape ribs into roasting pan or baking pan. Pour sauce over them and cover. Bake about 1 hour. Uncover and bake 15 –30 minutes longer, basting often.

Serve with parsley buttered potatoes and a green salad.

Serves 4.

Barbecue Sauce

3 tsp. peanut oil
2 cups onion, finely chopped
1 (1lb.) can imported plum tomatoes
1 cup ketchup or chili sauce
¼ cup white vinegar
¼ cup Worcestershire sauce
Salt to taste
1 tsp. ground black pepper
1 or 2 tbsp. chili powder
½ tsp. cayenne pepper, more or less to taste
1 ½ cups water
1 tsp. dried oregano
1 tsp. cumin powder
2 - 4 tbsp. honey

Heat oil in large, deep skillet and add onion. Cook, stirring often, until golden. Add remaining ingredients and bring to boil. Simmer, stirring frequently, about 45 minutes. Let stand overnight before using.

Makes 3 to 3 ½ cups sauce.

Beef Stew

The method calls for cooking at 250° for 6 hours, but this was before the day of the crock pot. Now use your crock pot.

2 lbs. stew meat
8 carrots, cut in coin shaped pieces
1 cup celery, cut in pieces
1 (29 oz.) can whole tomatoes
½ pkg. dry onion soup mix
4 oz. sherry
3 tbsp. tapioca
2 slices white bread, cubed
1 tbsp. salt
Pepper
Thyme
Marjoram
Rosemary (start with ¼ - ½ tsp. of each)
1 (10 oz.) pkg. frozen peas

Combine all ingredients except peas, and cook covered at 250° for 6 hours or place in crock pot and cook all day. Add peas last 30 minutes.

Serve with mashed potatoes and a green salad.

Serves 4 - 6.

Beef Stroganoff

3 lbs. top round steak - cut across grain into strips
1 large onion, chopped
1 clove garlic, minced
1 lb. fresh mushrooms
¼ cup dry red wine
1 can consommé, undiluted
1 tbsp. Worcestershire sauce
½ cup sour cream mixed with 1 tbsp. flour

Brown meat and put in a casserole. Add wine to the casserole. Sauté onion and mushrooms in same pan and add to casserole. Add the consommé and Worcestershire to casserole. Bake 1 ½ hours at 300° or until tender. Add the sour cream mixture at the end and heat through. Serve over cooked egg noodles.

Serves 6 - 8.

Casserole of Layers

3 potatoes, thinly sliced
1 medium onion, sliced
½ green pepper diced
2 slices bacon, diced
1 cup shredded Cheddar cheese
1 lb. ground beef, raw
3 tbsp. raw rice
1 can tomato soup
Salt and pepper

Layer in a 2 qt. casserole in the order given. Season layers with salt and pepper as you go. Cover all with 1 can tomato soup. Cover and bake 1 hour at 350º

Serves 6 - 8.

Chicken Divan

1 lg. bunch broccoli, cut into spears and steamed 2 minutes
then drained on paper towels
8 chicken breast halves, with bone and skin
1 can cream of chicken soup
1 cup mayonnaise
½ tsp. curry powder
1 tbsp. fresh lemon juice
½ cup bread crumbs
2 tbsp. melted butter
1 cup sharp Cheddar cheese, grated

Cook broccoli and drain. Cook chicken breasts. Debone chicken and remove skin. Mix soup, mayonnaise, lemon juice and curry powder together. Layer broccoli in 9 x 13 casserole. Top with chicken breasts. Spread soup mix over chicken. Mix bread crumbs and melted butter, add cheese and mix. Put over the sauce. Bake covered at 350° for 30 - 40 minutes. Uncover and bake 10-15 minutes longer. Can be made a day ahead and refrigerated before baking.

Serves 8.

Chicken Elegante

1 cut up fryer
¼ cup foaming butter
1 can cream of chicken soup
1 (4 oz.) can sliced mushrooms
½ cup sherry
Onion flakes
Salt and pepper

Brown chicken in butter. Place in casserole. In pan used to brown chicken, add soup, mushrooms, sherry, onion flakes and salt and pepper. Mix and heat through. Pour over chicken, cover and bake 2 hours at 300º.

Serves 4 - 6.

Chicken Escallope

1 (8 oz.) pkg. Pepperidge Farm stuffing
3 cups chicken, cut up
½ cup butter
½ cup flour
¼ tsp. salt and pepper
4 cups chicken broth
6 eggs, beaten
Bread crumbs, buttered
Mushrooms,optional

Gravy
1 can mushroom soup
¼ cup milk
1 cup sour cream
1 (2 oz.) jar pimento.

Make a sauce with the butter, flour, seasonings and chicken broth. Cool and add eggs. Mix stuffing per package directions. Put in well greased 9 x 13 pan. Put chicken on top. Add mushrooms, if desired. Spoon sauce over all and cover with buttered crumbs. Bake at 325º for 45 minutes to 1 hour.

Gravy
Mix ingredients and heat through before serving.

Serves 8.

Chicken in Phyllo

A real crowd pleaser!

6 large raw boneless, skinless chicken breasts, cut into 1"pieces
1 ½ cups mayonnaise
⅓ cup lemon juice, freshly squeezed
1 cup green onions, sliced
2 tsp. dried tarragon
2 garlic cloves, crushed
Salt and pepper
¾ lb. butter, melted for Phyllo dough
Parmesan cheese for tops, freshly grated
1 lb. box Phyllo dough, thawed

Mix together chicken, mayonnaise, lemon juice, green onion, tarragon, garlic, salt and pepper. Place a sheet of Phyllo dough on work space. Brush with melted butter. Add 1 more sheet of Phyllo on top. Place ⅛ of the chicken mixture on dough 2" from edge. Fold dough over the mixture, buttering each edge as you go. Place on cookie sheet and cover. Refrigerate or freeze. If frozen, start baking at 400º for 15 minutes. Turn oven to 350º and bake 20 minutes more, adding Parmesan for the last 10 minutes. If refrigerated, bake at 375º for 25 minutes adding Parmesan for the last 10 minutes.

Serves 8.

Chicken Kiev

1 (8 oz.) pkg. cream cheese, softened
1 egg yolk
Salt, cayenne pepper to taste
1 tsp. Worcestershire
1 tbsp. milk
6 oz. frozen crabmeat
12 skinless, boneless chicken breasts
2 eggs beaten
Dash of garlic powder
Club crackers, crushed
½ pt. sour cream
2 tbsp. Dijon mustard

Use a mallet to pound the chicken breasts and flatten. Mix the cream cheese, egg yolk, salt, pepper, Worcestershire, milk and crabmeat. Spread crab mixture in chicken breasts and roll. Secure with toothpicks. Refrigerate for several hours. Beat 2 eggs mixed with a little water and a dash of garlic powder. Dip chicken in egg mixture and roll in cracker crumbs. Sauté slowly in ½ cup margarine melted in skillet for about 25 minutes. Wine may be added, if desired, the last 5 minutes. Serve with sauce poured on top.

Sauce
Combine sour cream with mustard. Warm, but do not boil.

Serves 8-12.

Chicken Waikiki Beach

1 chicken, cut up
1 (1 lb. 4 oz.) can pineapple chunks - reserve juice
½ cup sugar
2 tbsp. cornstarch
⅜ cup cider vinegar
1 tbsp. soy sauce
¼ tsp. ground ginger
1 tsp. chicken bouillon
1 green pepper, sliced

Put chicken skin side up in baking pan. Add salt and pepper to taste and bake at 350° while making sauce. Drain pineapple and pour juice into a 2 cup measure. Add water to make 1¼ cups. Combine sugar, cornstarch, juice, vinegar, soy sauce, ginger and bouillon and bring to a boil stirring for 2 minutes. Pour over chicken and bake uncovered 30 minutes at 350°. Add green pepper and pineapple chunks and bake another 30 minutes or until tender. Serve with rice.

Serves 4.

Company Casserole

1 (6 oz.) pkg. long grain and wild rice mix
1 medium bunch broccoli, cut up and blanched
2 cups cooked chicken, diced
1 (4 oz.) can mushrooms
1 cup sharp Cheddar, grated
1 (8 oz.) can sliced water chestnuts
1 can cream of chicken soup
1 cup mayonnaise
2 tsp. mustard
⅓ tsp. curry
½ cup Parmesan cheese, grated

Cook rice according to package directions. Spread rice on bottom of greased 9 x 13 pan. Then layer broccoli, chicken, mushrooms and water chestnuts. Blend soup and mayonnaise with mustard and curry. Spread on top. Sprinkle with Cheddar cheese, then Parmesan. Bake at 350° for 45 minutes.

Serves 8.

Country Style Pork Chops

Delicious and easy!

4 pork chops
4 medium potatoes, peeled and sliced
2 medium onions, sliced
¼ cup butter
¼ cup flour
1 cup milk
½ tsp. salt
1 cup sour cream
1 ½ tsp. dry mustard

Brown chops. Arrange potatoes in a casserole, cover with onions and place chops on top. Make sauce with butter, flour, milk and salt. When thickened, add sour cream and mustard. Pour sauce over all and cover. Bake at 350° for an hour. Test chops for tenderness. Reduce heat to 300° and bake for another hour.

Serve with applesauce and fresh green beans.

Serves 4.

Evelyn's Easy Good Chicken

1 (3 lb.) fryer, cut up
1 can cream of chicken soup
½ cup half and half
¼ cup dry sherry
1 cup cooked rice
Accent
Salt
Lawry's salt
Paprika
Parsley

Arrange the chicken pieces skin side up in a 9 x 13 baking pan. Sprinkle with Accent and Lawry's salt. Combine the soup with the half and half and mix until smooth. Add the sherry to soup mix and pour over chicken. Sprinkle with paprika and parsley. Bake at 350º for an hour and a half. Then add the rice in and around the chicken pieces. Bake another half hour.

Serve with steamed broccoli and fruit salad or tossed salad with oil and vinegar dressing.

Serves 4 - 6.

Fu Man Chew

1 cup onion, chopped
1 tbsp. oil
2 cans cream of mushroom soup
1 cup raw rice
1 cup bean sprouts with liquid
1 (8 oz.) can sliced water chestnuts
4 tbsp. soy sauce
¼ tsp. salt and pepper to taste
1 (10 oz.) pkg. frozen pea pods, partially thawed
1 (3 oz.) can chow mein noodles
1 cup celery, chopped
2 lbs. ground beef

Sauté onion and celery in oil for 5 minutes. Add ground beef and brown. Add soup, rice, bean sprouts and liquid, water chestnuts, soy sauce, salt and pepper. Bake in 3 ½ quart casserole for 30 minutes at 350°. Add pea pods and top with noodles. Bake uncovered for 30 minutes more.

Serves 12.

Goulash

1 lb. ground sirloin
2 cups cooked shell macaroni
1 (8 oz.) can mushrooms
1 lg. onion, cut into quarters and sliced
½ green pepper, diced
1 tsp. salt
1 can tomato soup
Garlic powder
1 cup sharp Cheddar cheese, grated

Cook macaroni and drain. Set aside. Sauté meat, onion and mushrooms until meat is browned. Add macaroni and cool 5 minutes. Add green pepper, salt, soup and garlic powder. Mix well. Put in casserole and bake 30 minutes at 350°. Add cheese the last 10 minutes.

Serves 4-6.

Hot Chicken Casserole

1 can cream of chicken soup
1 cup mayonnaise - (can use Hellmann's Light)
1 tbsp. fresh lemon juice
1 small onion, chopped
1 box Uncle Ben's Wild Rice Mix (Original Recipe), cooked
3 cups cooked chicken or turkey, diced
1 ½ cups celery, diced
1 ½ cups (6oz.) sharp Cheddar cheese, grated
Toasted slivered almonds, if desired

Mix soup, mayonnaise and lemon juice. Add celery, onion, chicken and cooked rice. Stir to mix. Place in greased casserole (9 x 13 or equivalent) and bake at 350° for 30 minutes. Top with cheese and almonds and bake an additional 10 - 15 minutes.

Serves 6 - 8.

Italian Spaghetti Sauce

1 lb. bulk pork sausage
1 (29 oz.) can diced tomatoes
1 (6 oz.) can tomato paste
1 ½ medium onions, finely chopped
1 clove garlic, crushed
1 clove garlic, cut in 3rds
1 ½ tsp. sugar
¼ tsp. Tabasco sauce
Salt and pepper to taste.

Brown meat and pour off excess fat.
Add all other ingredients and simmer 1 hour.

Serves 4 - 6.

Macaroni Cheese Soufflé

1 cup elbow macaroni
2 cups milk
2 tbsp. butter
2 cups soft bread crumbs
2 cups process cheese, such as Velveeta or sharp Cheddar, cubed
2 tbsp. minced onion
20 stuffed olives, sliced
3 eggs, well beaten

Sauce-*optional*
1 can cream of mushroom soup
½ cup milk

Preheat oven to 350º. Grease a 1 ½ qt. casserole. Cook macaroni according to directions. In a small saucepan, heat the 2 cups milk with butter until butter melts and milk is scalded. In a large bowl combine drained macaroni, milk and butter, bread crumbs, cheese, onion and olives. Fold in the beaten eggs and pour into the prepared dish. Bake about 40 minutes. If desired, prepare sauce. In a small saucepan combine soup and the ½ cup milk, stirring well. Heat through and serve with soufflé.

Serves 8.

Meat Loaf

1 lb. ground round
½ medium onion, finely chopped
¼ cup oatmeal
½ cup milk
¼ cup ketchup
1 tsp. salt
1 ½ tsp. Worcestershire
Dash of Tabasco
Chili sauce

Mix all ingredients except chili sauce together and shape into loaf. Place in bread pan that has been sprayed with non-stick cooking spray. Spread chili sauce all over top of loaf. Bake at 325° for 1 hour.

Serves 4 - 6.

Mother's Lasagna

1 (8 oz.) pkg. lasagna noodles, cooked per package directions
1 lb. lean ground beef
½ lb. sweet Italian sausage
2 medium onions, chopped
1 clove garlic, crushed
2 tbsp. olive oil
1 (14-15 oz.) can Italian tomatoes
1 (12 oz.) can tomato paste
1 tsp. salt
½ tsp. oregano
Pepper
1 lb. ricotta cheese
1 egg
1 lb. mozzarella cheese
1 ½ cups Parmesan cheese

Brown onions and garlic in oil. Add ground beef and sausage and cook until done. Add tomatoes and tomato paste, salt, oregano and pepper. Simmer 30 minutes. Add beaten egg to ricotta cheese plus salt to taste. Grease 9 x 13 pan and cover the bottom with 1 ½ cup sauce. Top with a layer of noodles, ½ cup Parmesan, ½ of the ricotta cheese, ½ lb. thin sliced mozzarella cheese and some sauce. Repeat layer and the last layer will be noodles, sauce and Parmesan. Bake at 350º for 30 minutes. OR: Refrigerate, covered, overnight . Bake at 350º for 2 hours. Uncover for last 15 minutes. Let stand 15 minutes before cutting.

Serves 12.

Oriental Chicken

2 whole skinless, boneless chicken breasts
2 tbsp. oil
1 ½ cups fresh green beans
¼ tsp. ground ginger
1 ½ cups carrots, thinly sliced diagonally
1 ½ cups sliced fresh mushrooms
1 can cream of chicken soup
2 tbsp. sherry
1 tsp. soy sauce

Cut chicken in strips. Pour oil in fry pan and preheat on medium heat for 2 minutes. Add beans and ginger and cook 3 minutes. Stir constantly. Add chicken and carrots; cook 10 minutes stirring often. Push to side. Add more oil if necessary. Add mushrooms, cook 1 minute, stirring. Add soup, ¼ cup water, sherry and soy. Heat through, stirring often. Serve with rice.

Makes about 4 ½ cups.

Oriental Hot Dish

1 ½ lbs. ground beef or marinated chuck steak, cut in bite size pieces
2 cups celery, chopped
1 medium onion, chopped
2 tbsp. soy sauce
1 can mushroom soup
1 can chicken rice soup
1 (14 oz.) can oriental vegetables
2 cups chow mein noodles
½ cup sliced water chestnuts
½ cup sliced mushrooms

Brown meat, celery and onion. Add seasonings to taste and all the rest of the ingredients, saving ¾ cup noodles for top. Place in a greased 9 x 11 casserole. Bake at 350° for 45 minutes. Add the reserved noodles on top and bake enough longer to be bubbling at edges.

Serves 8.

Pasta Primavera

½ cup margarine
1 medium onion, chopped
1 clove garlic, crushed
1 lb. asparagus, cut diagonally
½ lb. mushrooms, sliced
6 oz. small broccoli florets
1 medium zucchini, cut into ¼" rounds
2 carrots, cut diagonally in ⅛" slices
1 cup whipping cream
½ cup chicken broth
2 tsp. dried basil
1 cup frozen tiny peas, thawed
8 oz. ham, chopped
5 green onions, chopped
1 lb. fettuccini or linguini, cooked al dente
Salt and pepper
1 cup Parmesan, grated

Heat a large, deep skillet and add margarine, onion, garlic. Sauté until onion is softened about 2 minutes. Add asparagus, mushrooms, broccoli, zucchini and carrot and stir fry 2 minutes. Increase heat to high. Add cream, broth and basil. Allow mixture to boil until liquid is slightly reduced. Stir in peas, ham and green onion and cook one minute. Season with salt and pepper. Add to hot pasta with cheese and toss. Turn onto serving platter and serve quickly.

Serves 4 - 6.

Priscilla's Macaroni and Cheese

1 (1 lb.) box medium size shell macaroni
2 (10 oz.) pkgs. extra sharp Cracker Barrel Cheddar cheese
¼ lb. butter or margarine
Salt and pepper
¼ - ½ cup milk

Cook macaroni and drain well. Slice the cheese. Grease a deep casserole thoroughly. Put in a layer of macaroni and dot with butter, salt and pepper. Cover the layer with slices of cheese, overlapping slices a little. Repeat with second and third layer. Pour milk into corners and a bit in the middle. Bake covered at 350° for 30 minutes. Uncover and bake another 20 - 30 minutes until the top is crispy.

Serves 6.

Roast Leg of Lamb

One half leg of lamb
Cider vinegar
½ cup flour
1 tbsp. dry mustard
1 tsp. salt
Freshly ground pepper
Rosemary
Red potatoes, peeled and cut into pieces

Moisten leg of lamb with cider vinegar. Blend dry ingredients and coat meat. Place in a roasting pan and roast at 325° for 1 hour. This coating keeps the juices in the meat. After 1 hour, place potatoes around the meat and baste with juices. Keep turning potatoes to brown evenly. Roast another hour or until done.
Serve with mint sauce.

Serves 4-8.

Shipwreck Stew

2 tbsp. margarine
2 medium onions, sliced
2 large potatoes, peeled and sliced
1 lb. ground chuck, crumbled
1 (15 ½ oz.) can kidney beans, drained
Scant ½ cup raw rice
1 cup celery, sliced
1 can tomato soup
½ cup water
1 ½ tsp. salt
1 tsp. chili powder
½ tsp. Worcestershire
¼ tsp. ground black pepper
Dash of cayenne
1 cup Cheddar cheese, grated

Grease large, heavy casserole with margarine. Layer in this order: onions, potatoes, ground chuck, kidney beans, rice, celery. Mix soup with water and seasonings and mix well. Pour over casserole. Cover tightly and bake at 350º for 1 ¼ hours. Remove cover and sprinkle with cheese. Bake uncovered until cheese melts. Flavor gets better next day.

Serves 6-8.

Sour Cream Noodle Bake

This is a family favorite!

1 (8oz.) pkg. egg noodles
1 lb. ground round
2 tbsp. butter or margarine
1 tsp. salt
⅛ tsp. pepper
¼ tsp. garlic salt
1 (8oz.) can tomato sauce
1 cup cottage cheese
1 cup sour cream
6 green onions, chopped
¾ cup shredded sharp Cheddar cheese

Cook noodles, rinse and drain. Brown meat in butter, add salt, pepper and garlic salt. Mix in tomato sauce, simmer 5 minutes. Combine cottage cheese, sour cream, green onions and noodles. Alternate layers beginning with the noodle mixture and then meat mixture. Top with Cheddar cheese. Bake 25 minutes at 350° until cheese melts.

Serves 6-8.

Spaghetti Pie

6 oz. spaghetti
2 tbsp. margarine
⅓ cup Parmesan cheese
2 well-beaten eggs
1 lb. ground beef
½ cup onion, chopped
¼ cup green pepper, chopped
1 (8 oz.) can tomatoes, cut up
1 (6 oz.) can tomato paste
1 tsp. sugar
1 tsp. oregano
1 tsp. garlic salt
1 cup cottage cheese
4 oz. shredded Monterey Jack cheese

Cook spaghetti and drain. Stir margarine into hot spaghetti, then Parmesan and eggs. Form mixture into a crust in a 10 inch pie plate. In skillet, cook ground beef, onion and green pepper until vegetables are tender. Drain off fat. Stir in undrained tomatoes, tomato paste, sugar, oregano and garlic salt. Heat through. Spread cottage cheese on spaghetti crust. Top pie with meat mixture. Bake uncovered at 350° for 20 minutes, or until bubbly. Sprinkle the cheese on top and bake until cheese melts.

Serves 4-6.

Stuffed Shells

18 - 20 jumbo shells for stuffing
1 ¼ lbs. ground beef
1 clove garlic, crushed
1 cup cottage cheese
1 cup shredded mozzarella or Monterey Jack cheese
½ tsp. salt
¼ cup mayonnaise
1 (15 ½ oz.) jar spaghetti sauce
⅓ cup Romano cheese, freshly grated

Cook and drain shells. Sauté beef and garlic. Remove from heat and add cottage cheese, mozzarella, salt and mayonnaise. Stuff shells with mixture and arrange in a greased 9 x 13 pan. Pour spaghetti sauce over shells. Sprinkle with Romano. Cover and bake at 350º for 15 minutes. Uncover and bake 10 minutes more.

Serves 6 - 8.

Swiss Corned Beef Scallop

2 cups Swiss cheese, grated
½ cup green onions, sliced-use tops too
1 tbsp. dried dill
2 tbsp. butter
2 tbsp. flour
1 tsp. salt
1 cup milk
1 cup sour cream
8 - 9 medium potatoes, cooked
2 - 3 cups corned beef, cooked and cubed
1 cup soft bread crumbs
¼ cup butter, melted

Mix 1 ½ cup Swiss cheese with dill and green onion. Make cream sauce with 2 tbsp. butter, flour and milk. Cook until thick. Remove from heat and stir in sour cream. Grease 3 qt. casserole. Peel and slice ⅓ of potatoes as bottom layer. Add ½ of the corned beef, ½ of Swiss cheese mixture and half the cream sauce. Repeat layers. Use last ⅓ of potatoes on top. Combine remaining Swiss cheese with bread crumbs and melted butter. Put on top. Bake at 350° about 35 minutes.

Serves 6 - 8.

Swiss Turkey Casserole

4 cups cooked turkey or chicken, cubed
2 cups celery, sliced
2 cups toasted bread cubes or stuffing cubes
1 cup mayonnaise
½ cup milk
1 tsp. salt
1/8 tsp. pepper
¼ cup or more onion, chopped
8 oz. Swiss cheese, grated

Mix mayonnaise, milk, salt and pepper. Add turkey, celery, bread cubes, onion and grated cheese. Mix well and bake in 9 x 13 greased casserole at 350° for 25 - 30 minutes uncovered.

Serves 6 - 8.

Tasty Chicken Casserole

1 (3 lb.) fryer
1 green pepper, cut in rings
2 onions, halved
4 small potatoes, halved
4 carrots, cut diagonally in 1" pieces
2 celery stalks, cut same as carrots
1 (16 oz.) can stewed tomatoes
Salt and pepper to taste
2 tbsp. margarine, melted
Paprika

In a large casserole, place whole chicken in center and arrange vegetables around it. Pour tomatoes over all and season with salt and pepper. Bake, covered, at 375° for an hour. Baste with pan juices. Brush melted margarine over the chicken and vegetables. Sprinkle with paprika. Bake until all is tender. Depending on your oven, use your own judgment about covering or leaving uncovered the last hour.

Fruit salad would be good with this.

Serves 4 - 6.

Turkey or Ham and Wild Rice Casserole

1 (6 oz.) pkg. long grain and wild rice mix
½ cup onion, chopped
½ cup celery, chopped
2 tbsp. butter or margarine
1 can mushroom soup
½ cup sour cream
½ tsp. curry powder
2 cups cooked turkey or ham
⅓ cup dry white wine
¼ cup parsley, snipped

Prepare rice according to package directions. Meanwhile, in pan, cook onion and celery in butter until tender, but not brown. Blend in soup, sour cream and curry. Stir in ham or turkey, the rice mix and the wine. Turn mixture into 12 x 7 x 2 baking dish. Bake uncovered at 350º for 35 - 40 minutes. Garnish with parsley.

Serves 6.

Wild Rice Company Casserole

2 cups raw wild rice
4 cups water
2 tsp. salt
2 lbs. ground beef
1 lb. fresh mushrooms, sliced
½ cup celery, chopped
1 cup onion, chopped
½ cup butter
½ cup black olives, drained and chopped
½ cup sliced water chestnuts
¼ cup soy sauce
2 cups sour cream
2 tsp. salt
¼ tsp. pepper
½ cup slivered almonds
Parsley, chopped

Wash wild rice. In covered pan, gently cook wild rice in water with salt for approximately 45 minutes. Drain rice. Brown ground beef; set aside. Sauté mushrooms, celery and onion in butter for 5 minutes. Combine soy sauce, sour cream, salt and pepper. Add cooked rice, beef, onion, mushrooms, celery, water chestnuts and olives. Place mixture in a casserole and bake at 350° for 1 hour uncovered. Add water if needed and season to taste. Stir several times. Garnish with almonds and parsley.

Serves 8.

Vegetables and Side Dishes

Vegetables are an important and colorful part of any lunch or dinner. There are so many things you can do with them and the seasons offer a variety of choices. Depending on personal preferences, you can get away from the ordinary and prepare the extraordinary such as Asparagus Parmesan, Creamed Onions, or Spinach Artichoke Casserole to name only a few. Vegetables make it possible to create many tasty combinations. Don't be afraid to try something new and different.

Asparagus Parmesan

Great company dish!

May be prepared ahead. Bring to room temperature before heating.
1 lb. asparagus
2 tbsp. butter
½ cup mayonnaise
¼ tsp. salt
⅛ tsp. pepper
⅛ tsp. dry mustard
Juice of ½ lemon
½ cup bread crumbs
½ cup Parmesan, grated

Cook asparagus until barely tender. Drain well and place in greased casserole. Melt butter. Heat until brown. Blend in mayonnaise, seasonings and lemon juice. Spread on top of asparagus. Sprinkle with bread crumbs and top with Parmesan. Bake uncovered at 375º for 20 - 30 minutes.

Serves 4.

Baked Tomatoes

5 large ripe tomatoes
1 large onion, chopped
4 tbsp. butter or margarine
½ cup dried bread crumbs
Salt and pepper
1 tbsp. brown sugar
2 tbsp. Parmesan cheese – or more, grated

Peel and thickly slice 4 tomatoes and put in casserole. Peel and dice the last tomato. Sauté onion in butter. Add diced tomato, bread crumbs, salt, pepper and brown sugar. Spread over the tomatoes. Top with Parmesan cheese and bake at 300° for 30 minutes.

Serves 4.

Baked Zucchini

2 tbsp. oil
4 medium zucchini, sliced thinly
½ cup dry bread crumbs
½ cup shredded Mozzarella cheese
¼ cup Parmesan cheese, grated
2 tbsp. butter, melted

Put oil in bottom of shallow casserole and place zucchini over it. Make a topping with the rest of the ingredients and put over the zucchini. Bake, uncovered, at 350º for 45 - 60 minutes. Can be prepared ahead and baked later.

Serves 4 - 6.

Cauliflower Au Gratin

1 medium head cauliflower, separated into florets
Salt and pepper to taste
1 cup sour cream
1 cup sharp Cheddar cheese, grated
2 tsp. sesame seeds, toasted

Cook florets in small amount of water until tender. Drain well. Place ½ in 1 qt. casserole. Season with salt and pepper. Spread with ½ cup sour cream and ½ cup cheese. Top with 1 tsp. sesame seeds. Repeat layer. Bake uncovered, at 350º until cheese melts and it is heated through - about 10 minutes.

Serves 6.

Cheesy Brussels Sprouts Bake

2 (10 oz.) pkgs. frozen brussel sprouts
2 eggs, slightly beaten
1 ½ cups (2 slices) soft bread crumbs
1 can cream of mushroom soup
½ cup sharp Cheddar cheese, grated
2 tbsp. onion, chopped
Dash of pepper
1 tbsp. butter, melted

Cook sprouts and drain. Cut into quarters. Mix eggs, ½ cup crumbs, soup, cheese, onion and pepper. Stir in sprouts. Place in 1 ½ qt. casserole and top with remaining crumbs mixed with melted butter. Bake at 350º for 50 - 55 minutes.

Serves 6 - 8.

Cheesy Zucchini Casserole

3 medium zucchini, sliced
1 large onion, thinly sliced
3 medium tomatoes, chopped
1 (8 oz.) can tomato sauce
1 tsp. oregano
1 tsp. marjoram
1 tsp. basil
1 (8 oz.) pkg. mozzarella, grated
¼ cup Parmesan cheese, grated
1 tbsp. parsley, chopped

In a lightly greased 2 qt. casserole, layer half of the zucchini, onion, tomatoes and tomato sauce. Sprinkle with ½ tsp. of the oregano, marjoram and basil. Sprinkle half of the mozzarella cheese over top. Repeat layer. Sprinkle top with Parmesan, parsley and paprika. Cover and refrigerate until cooking time. Bake at 350º for 1 ½ hours.

Serves 8.

Chinese Vegetables

2 tbsp. oil
1 medium onion, chopped
3 ribs celery, sliced
1 (10 oz.) pkg. frozen peas
½ (10 oz.) pkg. frozen pea pods
½ (14 oz.) can bean sprouts

Sauté onion and celery in oil for about 2 minutes. Add rest of ingredients and cook about 8 minutes longer until tender crisp and still green. Season to taste with salt.

Serves 4.

Creamed Onions

4 (10 oz.) bags white pearl onions
⅓ cup margarine
⅓ cup +1 tbsp. flour
1 tsp. salt
Pepper
1 cup chicken broth
⅓ cup sherry – not cooking sherry
1 ⅓ cups light cream
6 tbsp. Parmesan cheese, grated
Fresh parsley, snipped

Cook onions according to directions on bag. Skin and drain well. Set aside. Melt butter in medium saucepan over moderately low heat. Blend in flour, salt and pepper stirring constantly. Gradually stir in chicken broth, cream, sherry and cook, stirring constantly, until thickened and smooth. Stir in Parmesan and parsley and remove from heat. Add onions and pour in casserole. Bake at 350° until heated through. Can be made ahead and refrigerated.

Mother always served creamed onions with Thanksgiving dinner and these are delicious.

Serves 6 - 8.

Curried Corn Pudding

1 cup onion, finely chopped
3 tbsp. butter
1 tsp. curry powder
2 cups whole kernel corn, (drained well, if canned)
2 cups creamed corn
1 tsp. salt
½ tsp. sugar
2 cups light cream
3 eggs, slightly beaten
Sprigs of parsley

Sauté the onion with the butter and curry powder until onion is soft. Transfer the mixture to a large bowl and add the whole and creamed corn, salt, sugar, cream and eggs. Blend well. Pour the mixture into a well buttered 1 ¼ qt. soufflé dish and bake at 350° for 1 hour and 15 minutes, or until the top is puffed and golden. Garnish with parsley.

Serve with barbecued ribs, tossed salad and garlic bread.

Serves 6 - 8.

Easy Rutabaga Au Gratin

4 cups (about 2 lbs.) rutabaga, cooked and diced
Salt and pepper
1 (10 1/2oz.) can condensed cheese soup
¼ cup light cream
2 tbsp. butter, melted
1 cup soft bread crumbs
½ cup shredded Cheddar cheese
2 tbsp. Parmesan cheese, grated

Place cooked rutabaga in a 1½ qt. shallow casserole. Sprinkle with salt and pepper. Combine cheese soup and cream. Pour over rutabaga. Combine melted butter, crumbs and cheeses; sprinkle over rutabaga. Bake at 375º for 15-20 minutes until cheese is melted and crumbs are golden.

Serves 4 - 6.

Fried Tomatoes

4 large ripe tomatoes
4 slices toast
4 tbsp. margarine, divided
2 tbsp. flour
½ tsp. curry powder
Salt
½ cup milk

Slice tomatoes thickly, flour them and fry over medium heat in heavy pan in 2 tbsp. margarine. When browned on both sides, but not too soft, place on a platter covered with buttered toast. Keep warm. To pan, add two more tbsp. margarine and 2 tbsp. flour. When well blended, add ½ tsp. curry powder and salt to taste. Add milk (enough to make a gravy) and mix well. Pour over all on the platter and serve.

Good for a summer supper with ham and a green salad with a tart vinegar and oil dressing.

Serves 4.

Gingered Carrots

1 lb. carrots, peeled and cut
2 tsp. lemon juice
1 tsp. salt
½ tsp. ground ginger
Dash of black pepper
1 tsp. parsley flakes or fresh parsley
2 tbsp. butter or margarine

Peel and cut carrots into ½ inch thick rounds. Place in baking dish. Combine lemon juice and seasonings and toss with carrots. Dot carrots with butter. Cover and bake at 400º for 30 minutes or until carrots are tender.

Serves 4 - 6.

Green Beans and Mushrooms

1 lb. fresh green beans
2 tbsp. butter
1 small onion, chopped
1 cup fresh mushrooms, sliced
½ cup sour cream
1 tsp. dill
½ tsp. salt
Dash of pepper

Cook beans and drain. In skillet, sauté onion in butter 3 – 5 minutes. Add mushrooms and cook 2 more minutes. Add beans, sour cream, dill, salt and pepper. Heat through and serve.

Serves 6.

Monterey Zucchini Casserole

1 cup rice (3 cups cooked)
1 (4 oz.) can green chilies, drained
1 lb. Monterey Jack cheese, divided
3 medium zucchini, sliced ¼" thick and parboiled
3 large tomatoes, peeled and sliced
2 cups sour cream
1 tsp. oregano
1 tsp. garlic salt
4 tbsp. green pepper, chopped
4 tbsp. green onions, chopped
1 tbsp. parsley, chopped

Place cooked rice in a greased 9 x 13 glass baking dish. Add a layer of chilies, chopped or in strips. Cover with half of the cheese, sliced thinly. Then place zucchini slices over cheese and top with tomato slices. Mix sour cream with oregano, garlic salt, green pepper, onion and parsley. Spoon over tomatoes. Grate the remaining cheese and sprinkle over top. Bake uncovered at 350° for 30 minutes or until bubbly. This can be assembled ahead and refrigerated until baking. If refrigerated, increase baking time by 15 minutes.

Serves 10-12.

Mother's Baked Beans

1 can butter beans, drained
1 can lima beans, drained
1 can kidney beans, drained
2 cans B&M baked beans
1 lb. bacon, diced and cooked
3 medium Bermuda onions, chopped
½ cup vinegar
¾ cup brown sugar
½ tsp. garlic powder
½ tsp. dry mustard

Put beans and cooked bacon in a casserole. Chop onions and sauté in some of the bacon fat. Mix seasonings with onions and simmer for 15 minutes. Add onion mixture to beans and mix well. Cook, covered, at 350º for 1 ½ hours.

Serves 8 - 10.

Noodles with Sesame Dressing

1 (8 or 9 oz.) pkg. fine egg noodles, cooked until tender
2 tbsp. sesame oil
2 tbsp. soy sauce
1 tbsp. peanut oil
1 tbsp. rice vinegar or a little less wine or cider vinegar
1 tsp. sugar
½ tsp. salt or more to taste
1 medium clove garlic, finely minced
¼ cup sesame seeds, toasted
½ cup green onions, finely minced, both green and white parts
Optional - dash or two of Tabasco

Combine all dressing ingredients and toss with cooked noodles.

Can be served warm as a side dish and is excellent with chicken or chill and serve as a salad.

Serves 4.

Ratatouille

⅓ cup olive oil
1 medium onion, thinly sliced
2 cloves garlic, crushed
4 green peppers, cut in strips
1 large or 2 small eggplants, peeled and diced
2 medium zucchini, cut in ½ inch slices
4 medium tomatoes, peeled, seeded and chopped
Salt and pepper

Heat the oil in a deep skillet or Dutch oven and sauté onion and garlic until very lightly browned. Turn down heat and add rest of ingredients. Stir well, cover and simmer 40 minutes. Remove cover, raise heat and reduce liquid slightly for 10 minutes. Serve hot, cold or reheated.

Serves 10 - 12.

Red Cabbage

1 medium size red cabbage
1 or 2 tart apples, peeled and chopped
2 tbsp. butter
1 medium onion, sliced
1 or 2 cups water
½ cup red wine vinegar
½ cup sugar
1 tsp. salt
¼ tsp. pepper
2 cloves
1 bay leaf
Juice of ½ lemon
2 or 3 tbsp. flour

Wash cabbage and cut as for slaw. Heat butter in heavy saucepan and sauté onion and apples 3 or 4 minutes. Add water, sugar, vinegar and seasonings. Bring to a boil and add cabbage. Cover and let simmer about 45 minutes until just tender. Just before serving, sprinkle flour on top to absorb liquid. Mix and serve.

Serves 6 - 8.

Sautéed Cherry Tomatoes

3 tbsp. unsalted butter
3 tbsp. brown sugar
½ tsp. oregano
2 small onions, sliced
4 cups cherry tomatoes
½ tsp. salt
Freshly ground pepper
¼ cup parsley, minced for garnish

Melt butter in large skillet over medium high heat. Add brown sugar and oregano, mix well. Increase heat to high, add onions and tomatoes and cook 3 minutes, stirring frequently. DO NOT OVERCOOK. Tomatoes should retain texture. Season with salt and pepper. Transfer to serving bowl. Garnish with parsley.

Serves 6.

Scrumptious Carrots

1 lb. carrots, peeled
1 to 1 ½ tbsp. margarine
Sweet or sour cream
Lawry's salt, only a little
Dill weed to taste

Thinly slice carrots on the diagonal. Melt margarine in a heavy kettle, add carrots and cook on high for 1 minute. Turn down heat and steam until done (no water, no salt) Add cream, Lawry's salt and dill weed. Simmer gently until cream is absorbed.

Good with pot roast, mashed potatoes and a tossed salad.

Serves 4.

Simmered Autumn Vegetables

2 slices bacon, diced
1 rutabaga, peeled, quartered and sliced thinly
1 medium onion, sliced
1 potato, peeled and sliced
2 carrots, peeled and sliced
1 ½ cups beef broth
Salt and pepper to taste

In medium saucepan, fry bacon until crisp. Add vegetables and sauté until vegetables are lightly browned. Add broth and season to taste. Simmer until vegetables are tender, 15 to 18 minutes. Serve hot.

Serves 4 - 6.

Spinach Artichoke Casserole

1 (14 oz.) can artichoke hearts
1 (10 oz.) pkg. frozen chopped spinach
1 (4 oz.) cream cheese, softened
¼ cup butter, melted
1 tsp. salt
¼ tsp. pepper
1 tbsp. lemon juice
⅛ tsp. Worcestershire sauce
Ritz crackers for topping, crushed

Cook spinach. Drain in colander and squeeze liquid out with a spoon. Drain artichokes well and squeeze dry with paper towel. In a mixing bowl, put the cream cheese, butter and seasonings and mix with mixer. Fold in spinach and blend. Put artichokes in a casserole and top with the spinach mixture. Sprinkle with cracker crumbs. Bake at 350º for 20 - 30 minutes.

Serves 4.

Spinach Casserole

3 (10 oz.) pkgs. frozen chopped spinach
¼ cup butter
1 cup Pepperidge Farm stuffing
1 tbsp. lemon rind, grated
1 tbsp. onion, grated
1 (8 oz.) pkg. cream cheese
2 tbsp. sour cream

Cook and drain spinach. Blend cream cheese, sour cream, onion and lemon. Add spinach and mix. Put into greased casserole. Crush stuffing and mix with melted butter. Sprinkle on top and bake at 350º for 25 minutes.

Serves 5 - 6.

Spinach Pecan Bake

3 (10 oz.) pkgs. frozen chopped spinach
4 tbsp. butter
½ cup onions, finely chopped
1 cup half and half
⅓ cup dry bread crumbs
½ cup pecans, chopped coarsely
½ tsp. nutmeg
1 tsp. salt
⅛ tsp. pepper

Topping
¼ cup bread crumbs
2 tbsp. butter

Sauté the onion in 4 tbsp. of butter. Cook spinach, drain and combine with sautéed onion. Add rest of ingredients except topping. Place in casserole. Make topping and add to casserole. Bake at 350° for 30 minutes.

Serves 6 - 8.

Stir Fried Celery and Broccoli

1 bunch celery - use 6 ribs
1 medium bunch broccoli, florets and stems
¼ cup oil
1 clove garlic, crushed
1 large onion, cut in rings
3 tbsp. soy sauce
¾ tsp. ginger
⅛ tsp. pepper

Thinly slice celery on the diagonal. Cut broccoli into florets. Peel stems and cut in ½" slices, set aside. In large skillet, heat oil. Sauté garlic for 30 seconds over low heat, increase heat to high and add celery and broccoli florets and stems. Stir fry for 3 minutes. Add onion, soy sauce, ginger and pepper. Stir fry until vegetables are tender crisp, 2 or 3 minutes.

Serves 4.

Sunday Company Casserole

1 (16 oz.) bag frozen peas
2 (4 oz.) cans mushroom pieces (reserve liquid)
1 (8 oz.) can sliced water chestnuts
1 can cream of mushroom soup
½ lb. Cheddar cheese, grated
1 can French fried onion rings

Put frozen peas, mushrooms and water chestnuts in a 9 inch casserole. Mix some of the mushroom liquid into the soup and heat. Add to casserole and mix ingredients. Sprinkle cheese over top. Cover and bake at 350º for 30 minutes. Remove from oven and place onion rings over top. Bake uncovered for about 15 minutes longer.

Serves 4 - 6.

Potatoes and Rice

Potatoes are a comforting vegetable.
Whether mashed or in potato salad
they help fortify any meal.
Our recipe for Pittsburgh Potatoes
is unbeatable! Rice lends itself to
oriental food and curried dishes.
Then you have wild rice
that is so good in soups and casseroles.

Aristocratic Rice

3 cups cooked rice
¼ cup green onions, finely chopped
1 ½ cups large curd cottage cheese
1 clove garlic, crushed
1 cup sour cream
¼ cup milk
¼ tsp. Tabasco sauce
½ tsp. salt
½ cup Parmesan cheese, grated

Combine rice with green onion. Blend cottage cheese with rest of ingredients except Parmesan. Combine with rice and pour into a greased 1 ½ qt. casserole. Sprinkle with Parmesan cheese and bake at 350º for 25 minutes.

Serves 6.

Baked Hash Brown Potatoes

1 (16 oz.) bag frozen hash brown potatoes
1 pt. half and half
⅔ stick margarine
Salt,to taste
Parmesan cheese, grated

Thaw potatoes. Heat cream, margarine and salt together. Pour over potatoes in baking dish and sprinkle Parmesan on top. Bake at 325° for 1 hour.

Serves 6.

Baked Mashed Potatoes

12 potatoes, boiled and mashed
1 (8 oz.) pkg. cream cheese
1 (8 oz.) carton sour cream
¼ lb. butter or margarine
Salt and pepper to taste
Shredded Cheddar cheese

Mix all with warm potatoes. Top with shredded Cheddar cheese. Bake at 350° for 35 - 45 minutes. Freezes well.

Serves 10 - 12.

Deluxe Hash Browns

This is an excellent accompaniment for Roast Beef or Ham

1 (32 oz.) pkg. frozen hash brown potatoes
1 can cream of potato soup
1 can cream of celery soup
1 large onion, chopped
1 (8 oz.) carton sour cream
Salt
Pepper
Parsley flakes
Paprika
Shredded Cheddar cheese

Put potatoes, soups, onion, sour cream, salt, pepper in large mixing bowl. Let stand until you can mix together. Put in lightly greased 9 x 13 pan. Sprinkle with parsley flakes and paprika. Cover top with shredded cheese. Bake, uncovered, at 300° for 1 ½ hours.

Serves 12.

Green Chilies and Rice Casserole

¾ cup raw rice
2 cups sour cream
1 lb. Monterey Jack cheese, divided
2 (4 oz.) cans peeled green chili peppers (not hot ones)

Cook rice according to package directions. Cool and mix with sour cream. Season with salt if needed. Grease 9 x 9 inch pan and spread ½ the rice on bottom. Cut ½ the cheese into domino shaped pieces. Wrap as well as you can with drained strips of peppers. Use all of these for 2nd layer. Add remaining rice. Grate remaining half pound of cheese and use as the 4th layer. Bake, uncovered, at 350° for 30 minutes.

Serves 4 - 6.

Patrician Potatoes

4 cups mashed potatoes, about 6 medium potatoes
3 cups cottage cheese
¾ cup sour cream
1 ½ tbsp. onion, grated
2 tsp. salt
⅛ tsp. pepper
Butter, melted
½ cup almonds

Mash potatoes thoroughly. Add no milk or butter. Press cottage cheese through a sieve or process in a food processor until smooth. Mix potatoes and cheese. Add sour cream, onion, salt and pepper and mix well. Spoon into a shallow, greased 2 qt. casserole. Brush with melted butter. Bake at 350º for 30 minutes. Place under broiler to brown surface. Sprinkle with almonds.

Serves 8.

Pittsburgh Potatoes

8 lg. red potatoes, peeled and cubed
1 lg. onion, chopped
2 small jars diced pimentos, drained
2 cups heavy white sauce
1 (10 oz.) pkg. extra sharp Cracker Barrel Cheddar cheese, grated
Salt and pepper to taste.

Cook potatoes, onion and pimento in salted water to cover until potato is JUST tender. Don't overcook. Drain in colander. In a heavy sauce pan, make white sauce. Add cheese and stir until cheese melts. Remove from heat. Add potato mixture. Stir and add salt and pepper to taste. Put in casserole and heat ½ hour at 350º. This is best made a day or two ahead. If casserole is cold, bake 1 hour at 350º. Wonderful with ham or roast beef.

Serves 6 - 8.

Wild Rice Casserole

1 (6 oz.) box seasoned Uncle Ben's Long Grain and Wild Rice
1 can chicken broth (use amount stated on rice pkg.)
1 tbsp. lemon juice
½ tsp. dried tarragon
6 lg. mushrooms, finely chopped
4 tbsp. butter
¼ cup dry sherry
2 tbsp. parsley
½ cup pecans, coarsely chopped and toasted
Salt and pepper to taste

Prepare rice according to package directions, substituting chicken broth for water and omitting butter. Add lemon juice and tarragon. Mix well. Bring to boil, cover and simmer per package instructions. Sauté mushrooms in butter. Add salt and pepper, sherry and parsley. Add to cooked rice and put in casserole. Toast pecans for 10 minutes at 350º and then add to rice. Heat casserole at 250º for ½ hour.

Serves 4-6.

9

Bread and Rolls

Most people, today, do not take the time to make yeast rolls but these are well worth the effort. If it is a brunch you are hosting, try the raspberry coffee cake which has a touch of almond flavoring and can be made a day ahead of time. A couple of other tasty treats are Mother's famous orange rolls which are simple to make, but oh so good hot out of the oven. Mother's raisin bran muffin recipe, a very moist muffin with a cinnamon and brown sugar topping, is always a crowd pleaser.

Apple Nut Coffee Cake

½ cup margarine or butter
1 cup sugar
2 eggs
1 tsp. vanilla
2 cups sifted flour
1 tsp. baking powder
1 tsp. baking soda
¼ tsp. salt
1 cup sour cream
2 cups apple, peeled and finely chopped

For topping:
½ cup chopped walnuts or pecans
½ cup brown sugar
1 tsp. cinnamon
2 tbsp. butter, melted

Cake method

In mixing bowl, cream margarine or butter and sugar. Add eggs and vanilla and mix well. Sift together the flour, baking powder, baking soda and salt. Add to creamed mixture, alternately, with sour cream. Fold in apple and spread in greased 13 x 9 x 2 baking pan.

Topping method

Combine chopped nuts, brown sugar, cinnamon and butter. Sprinkle over batter.

Bake at 350° for 35 - 40 minutes.

Serves 12 - 16.

Blueberry Coffeecake

¾ cup sugar
¼ cup soft margarine
1 egg
½ cup milk
2 cups flour
2 tsp. baking powder
½ tsp. salt
2 cups fresh blueberries

Cinnamon topping
½ cup flour
½ cup sugar
½ tsp. cinnamon
¼ cup butter

For Coffeecake
Cream ¾ cup sugar and ¼ cup margarine.
Add egg and beat. Sift dry ingredients
together and add alternately with the milk.
Fold in the blueberries. Spread in a greased 9 x 9 pan.

For Topping
Mix flour, cinnamon and sugar together and cut in butter. Sprinkle on top of blueberry mixture. Bake at 375° for 25 - 35 minutes or until a toothpick thrust into the center comes out clean.

Serves 6 - 8.

Blueberry Muffins

1 cup sugar
¼ cup margarine
1 cup milk
1 egg
1 ⅓ cup flour
2 tsp. baking powder
¾ tsp. cinnamon
¾ tsp. nutmeg
½ tsp. vanilla
¼ tsp. salt
1 cup fresh blueberries

Preheat oven to 375°. Prepare muffin tin with paper liners. In bowl, cream sugar and margarine on low speed. Add milk, egg, ⅔ cup flour, baking powder, cinnamon, nutmeg, vanilla and salt and mix just until thoroughly blended. Gently mix in remaining ⅔ cup flour and fold in blueberries. Fill muffin tins ¾ full. Bake 20 - 30 minutes until golden brown.

Serves 12 - 16.

Cherry Muffins

2 cups flour
¾ cup sugar
2 tsp. baking powder
¼ tsp. salt
¾ cup milk
2 eggs, slightly beaten
2 tbsp. margarine, melted
2 cups pitted fresh tart cherries or (1 can (16 oz.) pie cherries, drained can be substituted)

Heat oven to 400º. Mix 1 ½ cups of the flour with sugar, baking powder and salt in medium size mixing bowl. Mix milk, eggs and butter in small bowl. Stir milk mixture into flour mixture until just moist. Toss cherries with remaining flour in small bowl and fold into the batter. Spoon batter into greased muffin cups, filling each ⅔ full. Bake until golden about 20 minutes. Remove from tin and serve warm.

Makes about 12- 16 muffins.

Dill Beer Bread

Glaze
1 egg
½ tsp. salt

Bread
3 cups flour
4 tsp. baking powder
3 tbsp. brown sugar
2 tsp. dill
1 ½ tsp. salt
½ tsp. baking soda
12 oz. beer at room temperature.

Grease loaf pan

For Glaze: using a food processor, insert steel blade in work bowl and mix egg with salt for 4 seconds. Set aside. Do not clean work bowl.

For Bread: combine flour and next five ingredients in work bowl and mix. Add half the beer, and blend using 4 on and off turns. Add rest of beer and mix until just blended. Put in pan and brush top with egg glaze. Bake 45 minutes at 350°.

Serve warm.

Makes 1 loaf.

No Beat and No Fail Popovers

2 eggs
1 cup milk
1 cup pre-sifted flour
½ tsp. salt

Break eggs into bowl and add rest of ingredients. Mix well with spoon, disregard lumps. Grease muffin cups well and fill them ¾ full. Set oven at 450° and immediately put popovers in cold oven. Bake 30 minutes. Serve warm.

Makes 6.

Orange Rolls

2 cans refrigerator biscuits—like Hungry Jack
1 orange
4 oz. butter or margarine, melted
¾ cup sugar

Grate orange rind and mix with sugar in small bowl. Squeeze orange juice and mix with melted butter. Dip each biscuit in butter mix and then into sugar mix. Place each biscuit in a greased ring mold side by side standing up. Bake at 350° for 35 - 40 minutes. After 20 minutes, place tin foil lightly over top of biscuits to prevent over browning and continue baking. Remove and immediately turn upside down on serving plate.

Makes 20 rolls.

Parmesan Loaf

1 (10 count) pkg. refrigerated biscuits
2 tbsp. margarine, melted
¼ cup Parmesan cheese, grated

Dip biscuits in melted margarine, then in cheese. Arrange overlapping in 2 rows on baking sheet. Bake at 450º for 8 - 10 minutes.

Serves 5 - 6.

Raisin Bran Muffins

This is a winner. Everyone likes them!

15 oz. raisin bran cereal
1 cup butter or margarine, melted
3 cups sugar
4 eggs
1 qt. buttermilk
5 cups flour
3 tsp. soda
2 tsp. salt
1 cup brown sugar
1 to 1 ½ tsp. cinnamon

Beat butter or margarine and 3 cups sugar until fluffy. Add eggs, one at a time. Sift flour, soda and salt together. Add flour mixture, alternately with buttermilk, until all are well blended. Fold in raisin bran. Fill paper lined muffin tins almost full. Mix the 1 cup brown sugar and cinnamon together and sprinkle on top. Bake at 350º for 25 - 30 minutes. This mixture will keep for 6 weeks in the refrigerator so you can bake a few any time you wish.

Makes 4 - 5 dozen.

Raspberry Cream Cheese Coffee Cake

This coffee cake is delicious and wonderful for brunch.

2 ¼ cups unbleached flour
¾ cup sugar
¾ cup margarine or butter
½ tsp. baking powder
½ tsp. baking soda
¼ tsp. salt
¾ cup sour cream
1 egg
1 tsp. almond extract
1 (8 oz.) pkg. cream cheese, softened
¼ cup sugar
1 egg
½ cup raspberry preserves
½ cup sliced almonds

Heat oven to 350°. Grease and flour bottom and sides of 9 or 10 inch springform pan. In large bowl, combine flour and ¾ cup sugar. Using pastry blender or fork, cut in margarine until mixture resembles coarse crumbs. Reserve 1 cup of crumb mixture. To remaining crumb mixture, add baking powder, baking soda, salt, sour cream, 1 egg and almond extract; blend well. Spread batter over bottom and two inches up sides of prepared pan. (Batter should be about ¼ inch thick on sides). In small bowl, combine cream cheese, ¼ cup sugar and 1 egg; blend well. Pour over batter in pan. Carefully spoon preserves evenly over cheese filling. In small bowl, combine 1 cup reserved crumbs and sliced almonds. Sprinkle over top. Bake at 350° for 45 to 55 minutes or until cream cheese filling is set and crust is deep golden brown. Cool 15 minutes. Remove sides of pan. Serve warm or cool. Cut into wedges. Refrigerate leftovers.

Serves 16.

Sticky Rolls

Easy and delicious!

1 (4 oz.) pkg. regular butterscotch pudding mix
1 cup chopped pecans
½ cup packed brown sugar
4 tbsp. butter or margarine, softened
1 tsp. cinnamon
1 (1 lb.) loaf frozen bread dough, thawed

In bowl, combine pudding mix, pecans, sugar, butter and cinnamon. Stir until crumbly. Cut bread in half lengthwise, then in 8 pieces crosswise, so you have 16 pieces. Grease 11 x 7 x 2 pan. Sprinkle ½ of topping onto bottom of pan. Arrange pieces of dough and sprinkle with remaining topping. Cover and let rise in warm place until almost double. Bake at 350° for 35 - 40 minutes. Turn out of pan immediately and serve warm.

Serves 8.

Yeast Rolls

1 cup warm water
1 cake yeast
3 eggs, beaten
½ cup sugar
½ cup margarine or butter, melted
4 ½ cups flour
1 tsp. salt

Mix all in order given. Let rise to double in size (about 3 hrs). Cut dough into 24 strips. Roll each strip into a 6 - 8 inch rope. Tie rope into a loose knot and place on a greased cookie sheet in a crescent shape. Let rise again on cookie sheet.
Bake at 425° for 10 - 12 minutes.

Makes 2 dozen.

Zucchini Bread

3 cups flour
1 tsp. salt
1 tsp. soda
3 tsp. cinnamon
¼ tsp. baking powder
3 eggs, beaten
2 cups sugar
3 tsp. vanilla
1 cup oil
3 cups zucchini, unpeeled and grated
1 cup chopped pecans or walnuts
¾ cup raisins, optional

Sift together the flour, salt, soda, cinnamon and baking powder. Beat eggs, add sugar, vanilla and oil. Mix well. Stir in grated zucchini. Add dry ingredients and blend. Stir in nuts and raisins. Use any size greased bread pan(s) and fill them half full. Bake at 350º for 1 hour. Reduce baking time for bread pans smaller than 9 x 5.

Makes 1 9 x 5 loaf.

Cookies and Bars

"A little taste of sweet" was always what mother said she desired after a meal. With all of the tasty possibilities, our mother developed a tradition with one of her friends to create a wide array of cookies and bars, divide them and then give them as gifts to others at holiday time. This tradition has been continued to this day by her daughters and her granddaughter. Whether it be the crowd favorite Rocky Road Bars or the elegant but much loved Lemon Drop Cookies, we hope you will find these recipes versatile and delicious.

Apple Dream Bars

1 ½ cups flour
1 cup sugar, divided
½ cup butter
2 ½ cups apples, peeled and sliced
½ tsp. cinnamon
1 cup brown sugar
¼ tsp. salt
½ cup coconut
½ cup chopped walnuts or pecans
2 tbsp. flour
3 eggs

Mix the flour with ½ cup sugar and ½ cup butter. Mix until crumbly. Pat into bottom of 9 x 13 pan. Arrange apple slices on crumble mixture. Cover with ½ cup sugar mixed with ½ tsp. cinnamon. Bake at 350° for 30 minutes or until apples are done. Mix together the rest of the ingredients and spread over the hot layer. Bake 20 minutes more. Cool before cutting.

Makes 32 bars.

Butter Pecan Turtle Cookies

Crust
2 cups flour
1 cup brown sugar
½ cup butter, softened
1 cup pecan halves

Caramel Layer
⅔ cup butter
½ cup brown sugar
1 cup milk chocolate chips

Preheat oven to 350°. Combine ingredients for crust. Mix at medium speed until well blended. Pat firmly into ungreased 9 x 13 pan. Sprinkle pecans evenly over unbaked crust. Prepare caramel layer. Combine brown sugar and butter. Bring to a boil over medium heat, stirring until entire surface bubbles. Boil ½ to 1 minute. Pour caramel layer evenly over pecans and crust. Bake at 350° for 18 - 22 minutes. Do not over bake. Caramel layer can be soft when you take it out of the oven. Immediately sprinkle with chips. Allow chips to melt slightly 2 - 3 minutes. Swirl chips as they melt. Do not spread. COOL. Cut into 3 - 4 dozen bars.

Makes 3 - 4 dozen bars.

Chocolate Krispie Drops

1 cup dates, finely chopped
1 cup powdered sugar
2 tbsp. butter, melted
1 cup Rice Krispies
1 cup peanut butter
1 (12 oz.) pkg. chocolate chips

Mix first 4 ingredients together. Add peanut butter and mix. Roll into small balls and chill. In double boiler, melt the chocolate chips. Dip balls in chocolate. Cover thoroughly with chocolate. Chill.
These freeze well.

Makes 4 dozen.

Chocolate Peanut Butter Bars

½ cup butter or margarine
½ cup peanut butter
½ cup sugar
½ cup brown sugar
1 egg
2 tbsp. water
1 ¼ cups flour
¾ tsp. baking soda
½ tsp. baking powder
¼ tsp. salt
2 (6 oz.) pkgs. chocolate chips
½ cup chopped nuts

Heat oven to 375°. Grease 9 x 13 pan. Cream butter, peanut butter, sugars and egg. Add water, flour, soda, baking powder and salt. Add 1 package chocolate chips. Spread in pan. Bake 20 minutes. Remove from oven. Sprinkle remaining chips on top. When melted, spread evenly over top. Sprinkle with nuts.

Makes 32 bars.

Cinnamon Bars

1 cup butter
1 cup sugar
1 egg, separated
2 tsp. cinnamon
2 cups flour, sparingly
48 pecan halves

Cream butter and sugar. Add egg yolk, cinnamon and flour. Flatten dough on a large cookie sheet with palm of hand. Beat egg white with whisk and brush over top of dough. Score dough into squares and place pecan half on each square. Bake at 350º for 15 minutes. Remove from cookie sheet immediately.

Makes 4 dozen bars.

Cornflake Cookies

1 cup butter
1 cup sugar
1 tsp. baking soda
1 ½ cups flour
1 tsp. cream of tartar
1 tsp. vanilla
½ cup pecans, broken
2 cups corn flakes

Cream butter and sugar. Add baking soda, flour, cream of tartar and vanilla. Fold in pecans and corn flakes. Drop on ungreased cookie sheet. Bake at 350° for 10 - 12 minutes.

Makes 5 dozen.

Cranberry Tarts

Dough
½ cup butter or margarine, softened
½ cup sugar
1 egg
1 tsp. vanilla extract
2 cups all-purpose flour, unsifted

Filling
¼ cup butter or margarine
1 cup powdered sugar
½ cup dark corn syrup
½ cup chopped pecans
1 cup fresh cranberries, coarsely chopped

For Dough
In a large bowl with electric mixer at medium speed, combine butter or margarine, sugar, egg and vanilla until blended. Reduce speed to low; add flour and continue mixing until just well blended. Shape dough into a ball. Wrap with plastic wrap and chill 30 minutes. Meanwhile, make filling; set aside.

For Filling
Combine butter or margarine, powdered sugar and corn syrup in a small pan. Over medium heat, bring to a boil, stirring constantly. Boil 1 minute. Remove from heat and stir in pecans and cranberries. Set aside.

Preheat oven to 400°. On floured surface, roll dough to about ⅛ inch thickness. Using a 2 ¼ inch round cookie cutter, cut into circles.
Re-roll scraps. Press evenly into 1 ¾ inch tartlet or small cup cake pans. Bake 8 - 10 minutes until edges are lightly browned. Reduce oven to 350°. Spoon filling into partially baked shells. Return to oven. Bake for 10 - 12 minutes. Remove from pan as soon as possible.

Makes 4 dozen.

English Toffee Bars

1 cup butter
1 cup brown sugar
1 ½ cups flour
1 egg yolk
1 tsp. vanilla
6 Hershey Bars
Chopped walnuts or pecans

Cream butter and sugar. Add egg yolk and vanilla. Mix in flour. Spread on small cookie sheet. Bake 15 minutes at 350º. Remove from oven and cover with Hershey bars. Let the chocolate melt a little and spread evenly. Sprinkle with nuts. Allow chocolate to set, cut into squares and refrigerate.

Makes 5 dozen bars.

Fruit-Nut Brandy Drop Cookies

2 cups brown sugar
1 cup butter
4 eggs, well beaten
4 oz. brandy
2 tbsp. milk
3 cups flour
3 scant tsp. baking soda
1 tsp. cinnamon
1 tsp. nutmeg
½ tsp. salt
1 ½ lb. raisins
1 ½ lb. pecans, chopped

Cream butter and sugar. Add beaten eggs. Sift dry ingredients. Add dry ingredients to egg mixture alternately with the milk and brandy. Fold in raisins and pecans. Drop by small spoonfuls on greased cookie sheet. Bake at 350° for 15 minutes. Cool. If desired, decorate top with halves of candied cherries (before baking) to make a Christmas cookie. Freezes well.

Makes 10 dozen.

Lemon Drop Cookies

A wonderful tea cookie. They melt in your mouth!

Cookie

½ lb. butter
½ cup confectioner's sugar
2 cups flour

Lemon Curd

1 egg, beaten
¾ cup sugar
1 ½ tbsp. butter
3 tbsp. fresh lemon juice
Rind of 1 lemon, grated
Confectioner's sugar

For Cookie

Combine butter, confectioner's sugar and flour. Mix well. Roll into small balls. Make a thumbprint in the center of each ball. Place on greased cookie sheets. Bake in preheated 350º oven 10 - 12 minutes. Remove to rack and cool.

For Lemon Curd

In saucepan, combine all curd ingredients. Cook, stirring until thick. Cool. Spoon curd into thumbprint of each cookie. Sprinkle with confectioner's sugar. This curd may also be used as ice cream topping or combined with fresh pineapple, oranges and coconut.

Makes 50 - 60 cookies.

Monster Cookies

12 eggs
2 lb. brown sugar
4 cups white sugar
1 tbsp. vanilla
1 tbsp. light corn syrup
1 lb. butter
3 lb. peanut butter
8 tsp. baking soda
18 cups oatmeal
1 lb. chocolate chips
1 lb. M and M's

Cream butter and sugar. Add eggs, one at a time, beating after each addition. Add vanilla, corn syrup, peanut butter and baking soda. Mix well with electric mixer. Add oatmeal and mix by hand. Add chocolate chips and M & M's and mix by hand until well blended. Drop on cookie sheet and flatten slightly. Bake 8 - 10 minutes at 350º. Do not over bake. Can drop, using ice cream scoop, to make monster size and bake 12 minutes. Recipe can easily be divided in ½, or ¼ to make fewer cookies.

Makes 20 dozen cookies.

Peanut Butter Bars

1 cup margarine, melted
1 cup peanut butter
⅓ (14 oz.) box of graham crackers, crushed
1 lb. powdered sugar
1 (12 oz.) pkg. chocolate chips
1 tbsp. butter, melted

Mix first four ingredients together. Pat in cookie sheet. Melt chocolate chips over low heat with 1 tbsp. butter. If mixture is not spreadable, add more margarine until smooth. Spread over the peanut butter mixture. Refrigerate and cut into bars.

Makes 60 bars.

Peanut Clusters

2 lbs. white chocolate bark
1 (12 oz.) pkg. semi-sweet chocolate bits
1 (12 oz.) pkg. sweet chocolate bits
12 oz. German chocolate
4 (12 oz.) cans Planter's cocktail peanuts.

Place bark, chocolate bits and German chocolate in large oven-proof bowl. Place bowl in 200° oven to melt ingredients together. Remove from oven and stir in peanuts. Drop mixture from spoon onto waxed paper. Chill.

Makes 5 dozen.

Pecan Dreams

½ lb. butter
1 cup powdered sugar
2 cups flour, sifted
2 cups chopped pecans
2 tsp. vanilla
2 tsp. water.

Cream butter and sugar thoroughly. Add flour, vanilla and water and mix well. Fold in pecans. Chill and roll into balls. Bake at 250º for 30 - 40 minutes. Roll in powdered sugar while warm.

Makes 4 dozen.

Pumpkin Bars

Bars
4 eggs
1 cup oil
2 cups sugar
1 (15 oz.) can pumpkin
2 cups flour
2 tsp. baking powder
1 tsp. baking soda
½ tsp. salt
2 tsp. cinnamon
½ tsp. ginger
½ tsp. cloves
½ tsp. nutmeg

Frosting
6 oz. cream cheese, softened
1 tbsp. cream
6 tbsp. butter
1 tsp. vanilla
1 lb. powdered sugar, approximately

For Bars
Mix first four ingredients together in large bowl. Sift together the rest of the ingredients and stir into mixture in bowl. Pour onto greased and floured cookie sheet 12 x 18 x 1. Bake at 350º for 25 - 30 minutes. Cool and frost with cream cheese frosting.

For Frosting
Cream first four ingredients together and add powdered sugar, a little at a time, until mixture is smooth and easy to spread.

Makes 48 bars.

Rocky Road Bars

Made with two layers and frosting these bars are well worth the effort. Everyone loves them.

First layer

1/2 cup butter or margarine
2 oz. unsweetened chocolate squares
1 cup sugar
1 cup flour
2 eggs
1 tsp. baking powder
1 tsp. vanilla

In heavy saucepan, over low heat, melt butter and chocolate. Remove from heat and whisk in the remaining ingredients. Mix well and spread in greased 9 x 13 pan.

Second layer

8 oz. cream cheese, divided (save 2 oz. for frosting)
½ cup sugar
2 tbsp. flour
¼ cup soft butter or margarine
1 egg
1 tsp. vanilla
6 oz. chocolate chips

Soften 6 oz. cream cheese and cream with butter. Add egg, sugar, flour and vanilla. Spread mixture over first layer. Sprinkle with chocolate chips and bake at 350° for 20 - 25 minutes. Cool.

Continued on page 184....Frosting

Frosting

¼ cup butter or margarine
1 ½ oz. unsweetened chocolate
2 oz. cream cheese
¼ cup milk
3 cups powdered sugar
1 tsp. vanilla
2 cups miniature marshmallows

In pan, over low heat, melt butter, chocolate, cream cheese and milk. Remove from heat and add powdered sugar and vanilla. Mix well with a whisk. Return to heat and add marshmallows. Mix until smooth. Spread over cooled bars. Refrigerate at least over night before cutting into bars.

Makes 54 bars.

Tingalings

1 (6 oz.) pkg. chocolate chips
1 (6 oz.) pkg. butterscotch chips
1 ⅓ cup salted peanuts
1 ⅓ cup chow mein noodles

Melt chips in a double boiler over low heat. Put peanuts and noodles in a large bowl. Remove melted chips from heat and add to bowl. Mix well. Line cookie sheet(s) with plastic wrap. Use a spoon and drop onto cookie sheet. Chill. Freezes well.

Makes 4 dozen.

Treasure Chest Bars

Bars

½ cup butter or margarine
½ cup brown sugar
½ cup granulated sugar
2 eggs
1 tsp. vanilla
¾ cup milk
2 cups flour
1 ½ tsp. baking powder
1 tsp. salt
1 (8 oz.) jar maraschino cherries, drained and quartered (reserve liquid)
1 cup chopped walnuts or pecans
1 (6 oz.) pkg. chocolate chips

Frosting

¼ cup margarine or butter
2 cups powdered sugar
2 tbsp. milk
Reserved cherry juice

For Bars

Cream butter and sugars. Beat in eggs and vanilla. Alternately add milk and dry ingredients. Beat until smooth. Fold in nuts, cherries and chocolate chips. Pour into greased 9 x 13 pan. Bake at 325° for 35 - 40 minutes, or until done.

For Frosting

Melt margarine until golden brown. Remove from heat. Stir in powdered sugar, milk and small amount of reserved cherry juice to make a smooth glaze. Spread over warm cake. Can be frozen.

Makes 48 bars.

Yum Yum Bars

1 pkg. German Chocolate cake mix
¾ cup butter, melted
⅔ cup Carnation milk, divided
1 cup chopped walnuts or pecans
1 (6 oz.) pkg. chocolate chips
50 caramels

Mix the cake mix with the melted butter and ⅓ cup Carnation milk. Add chopped nuts and mix. Spread ½ batter in a 9 x 13 pan and bake at 350° for 6 minutes. Add chocolate chips on top. Melt caramels with remaining ⅓ cup Carnation milk. Drizzle over chocolate chips. Add rest of batter. Bake again at 350° for 15 - 18 minutes. Cool slightly and refrigerate to set the caramel. Cut into bars.

Makes 32 bars.

Desserts

In our family, no meal was complete without dessert. Mother took great care to select the perfect ending to our meal. Included in this selection, are recipes which are family fare such as Mother's cinnamon raisin bread pudding for which she was renowned. Others are show stopping desserts for dinner parties or special occasions such as the Chocolate Mousse Cake. If you are looking for the perfect holiday dessert, try Peace Pie, a lovely combination of pumpkin and mincemeat or Cranberry Christmas Cake. May you find these recipes as delicious as we do.

Apple Dapple Cake

Cake

1 ½ cups oil
2 cups sugar
1 tsp. vanilla
3 eggs
3 cups flour
1 tsp. salt
1 tsp. baking soda
4 cups apple, chopped with skins left on
1 ½ cups chopped walnuts or pecans

Sauce

1 stick margarine
1 cup brown sugar
¼ cup milk

For Cake

Mix first four ingredients together. Add flour, salt and soda. Fold in apples and nuts. Prepare a bundt pan by greasing and flouring thoroughly. Pour mixture into prepared pan and bake at 350° for 1 hour and 10 - 15 minutes. Turn cake out on serving plate. Cool.

For Sauce

Cook all ingredients for 3 minutes or until well blended. Spoon it over the cake. Wonderful, served warm, with vanilla ice cream. Also good for breakfast as a coffeecake! Can be easily frozen.

Serves 16 - 20.

Apple Pudding Cake

Pudding

1 cup sugar
¼ cup margarine
1 egg
2 ½ cups apple, unpeeled and chopped
1 tsp. baking soda
1 cup flour
¼ tsp. salt
1 tsp. cinnamon
1 tsp. nutmeg

Sauce

1 cup half and half
½ cup margarine
1 cup sugar
1 tsp. vanilla

For Apple Pudding Cake

Cream margarine, add sugar, egg. Blend in dry ingredients. Fold in apples. Pour into greased and floured 8 x 8 x 2 pan. Bake at 350º for 35 - 40 minutes. Serve with warm sauce. Sauce can be made ahead and re-heated.

For Sauce

In a saucepan, melt margarine. Whisk in sugar, half and half and vanilla. Cook for 3 minutes. Thicken with 1 tbsp. cornstarch, softened in a little cream.

Serves 9.

Bananas Brennan

¾ cup brown sugar
4 tbsp. butter
½ oz. banana liqueur
1 oz. rum
4 bananas, peeled and halved lengthwise
Vanilla ice cream, made into balls

Melt brown sugar and butter in top of chafing dish until bubbly.
Add the liqueur and rum (which you have warmed) and the bananas.
Flame and spoon over ice cream balls (which you have made ahead)
Very showy to do at the table for guests.

Serves 6.

Banana Split Pie

Pie

3 medium bananas
1 tbsp. lemon juice
1 9 inch baked pie shell
1 qt. strawberry ice cream
1 cup frozen whipped topping, thawed
Maraschino cherries
2 tbsp. finely chopped walnuts

Fudge Sauce

1 (6 oz.) pkg. chocolate chips
6 oz. evaporated milk
½ (1 pt.) jar of marshmallow crème

For Pie

Thinly slice the bananas, sprinkle with lemon juice and arrange on bottom of pie shell. Soften the ice cream slightly and spread atop bananas. Freeze until firm. Spread thawed topping over ice cream. Top with cherries and sprinkle with walnuts. Freeze again. Let stand 30 minutes at room temperature before serving. Serve with fudge sauce.

For Fudge Sauce

In sauce pan, combine the chocolate chips and the evaporated milk. Cook and stir over low heat until well combined. Beat in ½ of a 1 pint jar marshmallow crème, until mixture is well blended. Serve warm over pie. Makes two cups.

Serves 8.

Blueberry Cheese Cake Pie

17 graham crackers, crushed
⅓ cup butter, melted
¼ cup sugar
6 oz. cream cheese, softened
2 eggs
⅓ cup sugar
1 can blueberries in heavy syrup (reserve syrup)
1 ½ tbsp. cornstarch
⅓ cup sugar
1 ½ tbsp. lemon juice
Whipped cream

Make graham cracker crust with first three ingredients. Press into pie pan and bake 10 minutes at 325º. Mix cream cheese, eggs and ⅓ cup sugar and beat until fluffy. Spread mixture over cooled crust and bake at 375º for 20 minutes and let cool. Strain juice from blueberries and thicken with cornstarch and ⅓ cup sugar. Add blueberries and lemon juice. Mix well. Spread blueberry mixture over the pie. Refrigerate. Serve with whipped cream.

Serves 6 - 8.

Buster Bar Dessert

2 cups powdered sugar
1 ½ cup evaporated milk
1 cup chocolate chips
½ cup margarine
1 tsp. vanilla
1 lb. Oreo cookies
½ cup margarine, melted
1 ½ cups Spanish peanuts
½ gallon vanilla ice cream, softened

Mix powdered sugar, evaporated milk, chocolate chips, margarine and vanilla. Boil 8 minutes, stirring constantly to make chocolate sauce. Cool. Crush cookies and add melted margarine. Spread crumbs in 9 x 13 pan. Put peanuts over crumb crust and refrigerate. When set, put ice cream over peanuts. Cover with cooled chocolate sauce and freeze overnight.

Serves 12.

Candy Bar Pie

1 (9 oz.) box Nabisco Famous Chocolate Wafers
6 tbsp. butter or margarine, melted
1 tsp. instant coffee powder
2 tbsp. water
8 oz. Hershey Chocolate bars with almonds, broken into pieces
4 cups frozen whipped topping, thawed

Use ⅔ of the box of cookies and finely crush them. Mix with melted butter. Press into 9 inch pie pan and bake at 350º for 10 minutes. Cool well before filling. In small pan, dissolve coffee powder in water. Add broken chocolate, stir over low heat until melted. Cool. Fold in whipped topping and pile into crust. Freeze several hours or overnight. Top with real whipped cream or more whipped topping and chocolate shavings. Men really love this pie.

Serves 6 - 8.

Chocolate Cherry Cake

⅓ cup butter
1 egg, unbeaten
1 cup sugar
1 square unsweetened chocolate, melted
¼ cup maraschino cherry juice
¾ cup buttermilk
1 ½ cup cake flour
1 tsp. baking soda
¾ tsp. salt
½ cup maraschino cherries, cut up and floured

Cream butter and sugar. Add egg and mix. Add melted chocolate. Alternately add dry ingredients and liquid. Fold in cherries. Grease an 8 inch square pan. Add mixture and bake at 350º for 45 minutes. Top with your favorite chocolate frosting.

Serves 6 - 8.

Chocolate-Cherry Sundae Cake

Great for a summer dessert or a birthday party!

2 qts. vanilla ice cream
1 qt. chocolate ice cream
2 (9 inch) chocolate cake layers (made from mix)
1 (8 oz.) jar cherry preserves
1 pint whipping cream

Soften ice cream 1 qt. at a time and spread in a foil lined cake pan. Freeze. Split each cake layer in half so you have 4 layers. Place one cake layer on a plate. Unmold a vanilla ice cream layer on top of cake and spread with ⅓ of the cherry preserves. Top with another cake layer. Freeze. Do likewise with the other two layers. Freeze. When both are frozen, put together with chocolate ice cream layer in the center. Refreeze. Whip cream and frost sides and top of cake. Keep frozen until ready to serve.

Serves 12 - 16.

Chocolate Mousse Cake

10 oz. semi sweet chocolate (can use chips)
1 tsp. instant coffee
1 ¼ cups unsalted butter
1 ½ cups sugar
10 eggs, separated
1 oz. chocolate for curls
Whipped cream
9 inch spring form pan

Melt chocolate in double boiler over very low heat. Cool. Dissolve instant coffee in 1 tsp. water in microwave for 15 seconds. Beat butter and sugar until creamy. Add melted chocolate and coffee. Add egg yolks one at a time beating over a 15 minute period. In separate bowl, beat egg whites until stiff. Fold into chocolate mixture. Pour ¾ batter in greased spring form pan and bake 40 minutes at 350°. Cool. Center of cake will fall. Spread remaining batter in center. Refrigerate at least 24 hours. Can freeze.

To serve, frost with whipped cream and top with chocolate curls. This dessert is gluten free and very delicious. It is a show stopper for a dinner party!

Serves 12-16.

Chocolate Pound Cake

Cake
½ lb. butter
1 stick margarine
3 cups sugar
3 cups flour
½ cup cocoa
½ tsp. baking powder
¼ tsp. salt
5 eggs
1 cup milk
2 tsp. vanilla

Chocolate Buttercream Frosting
¼ cup butter
¼ tsp. salt
½ cup unsweetened cocoa
⅓ cup milk
2 tsp. vanilla or brandy or rum
3 ½ cups powdered sugar

For Cake
Cream butter, margarine and sugar until fluffy. Add eggs, one at a time, beating well after each addition. Sift together flour, cocoa, baking powder and salt. Combine milk and vanilla. Alternately add milk mixture and flour mixture to the creamed mixture. Pour into a greased and floured bundt pan. Bake at 325° for 80 - 95 minutes or until it tests done. Cool in pan 15 minutes. Cool on a rack out of pan at least an hour before frosting. Freezes well.

For Chocolate Buttercream Frosting
Cream butter and add cocoa, salt and flavoring. Add sugar slowly, alternating with milk until frosting is of spreading consistency.

Serves 16.

Cranberry Apple Nut Pie

2 (9 inch) pie crusts
2 cups fresh cranberries, coarsely chopped
2 cups apple, peeled and coarsely chopped
1-1 ½ cups sugar depending on the tartness of apples
½ cup walnuts or pecans, chopped
1-2 tbsp. quick tapioca
½ tsp. cinnamon
1 egg white, beaten

Combine cranberries, apples, sugar, nuts, cinnamon and tapioca. Let stand 20 minutes. Turn into piecrust after brushing inside with beaten egg white to keep crust from getting soggy. Place top crust on and flute edges as desired. Cut slits in top crust. (Optional. Brush top crust with milk and sprinkle with sugar.) Cover edge of pie with foil to prevent over browning. Bake at 375º for 25 minutes, then remove foil and bake for 20 - 30 minutes more until golden.

Serves 8.

Cranberry Christmas Cake

Cake

3 tbsp. butter
1 cup sugar
2 cups flour
1 cup milk
3 tsp. baking powder
¼ tsp. salt
3 cups fresh cranberries

Butter Sauce

1 cup sugar
1 tbsp. flour
½ cup butter
½ cup half and half
1 tbsp. vinegar
1 tsp. vanilla

For Cake

Beat together all ingredients, except cranberries. Fold in cranberries. Spread batter evenly in greased 8 inch or 9 inch square pan. Bake 35 - 40 minutes at 350º. Serve with butter sauce.

For Butter Sauce

Mix flour and sugar. Put all, except vanilla, in saucepan. Heat and stir until bubbly and cooked. Keep hot over hot water until serving. Add vanilla and serve over cake.

Serves 9.

Cranberry Pecan Pie

1 (9 inch) unbaked pie shell
2 cups whole cranberries
3 eggs
⅔ cup brown sugar
⅔ cup sugar
⅛ tsp. salt
1 cup light corn syrup
¼ cup butter or margarine, melted
1 cup pecan pieces

Heat oven to 325°. Place cranberries evenly in pie shell. Beat eggs. Add sugars, salt, corn syrup and butter. Mix well and pour over cranberries. Sprinkle pecan pieces evenly over top. Bake at 325° for 50 - 60 minutes or until knife inserted in center comes out clean. Serve with whipped cream.

Serves 8.

Derby Pie

Pie

1 cup sugar
4 tbsp. cornstarch
2 eggs, lightly beaten
½ cup butter or margarine, melted and cooled
3 tbsp. bourbon or 1 tsp. vanilla
1 (6 oz.) pkg. chocolate chips
1 cup chopped pecans
1 (9 inch) unbaked pie shell
Whipped cream

For Pie

Combine 1 cup sugar and cornstarch in medium bowl. Beat in eggs. Mix in butter, bourbon, chocolate chips and pecans. Pour into pastry shell. Bake at 350º for 40 minutes or until puffy and lightly browned. Cool.

Derby pie freezes well. When pie is cool, wrap and freeze. To serve, set unwrapped but frozen pie in 300º oven for 35 - 40 minutes. Serve slim wedges with whipped cream.

Serves 8 - 10.

Flaming Pineapple Dessert

1 fresh pineapple
½ cup sugar
1 tsp. cinnamon
¼ cup dark rum
½ cup macadamia nuts or cashews
Ice cream balls that have been rolled in coconut and refrozen
Cognac or brandy, warmed

Cut top off pineapple and save. Core and hollow out shell. Cut pineapple into small cubes and marinate in mixture of sugar, cinnamon and rum. Marinate 1 hour. Stir at least once. Refill shell with marinated fruit. Cover shell with foil (leave top off). Bake ½ hour at 350°. Remove foil, put on platter, add top, and take to table. Remove top, pour warmed Cognac or brandy over fruit and flame it. Serve over ice cream balls and sprinkle with nuts.

Serves 6 - 8.

French Silk Chocolate Pie

Pie Shell

1 cup sifted flour
½ tsp. salt
⅓ cup lard
2-3 tbsp. cold water

Filling

½ cup butter
1 cup sugar
2 squares unsweetened chocolate, melted and cooled
1 tsp. vanilla
2 eggs
1 cup whipping cream, whipped

For Pie Shell

Sift flour and salt together. Cut in shortening (can use food processor) until particles are like small peas. Add water and mix again. If dough is very soft, put in freezer for 20 minutes and then roll out to fit in an 8 inch pie pan. Prick crust with fork. To ensure crust does not crumble while baking, you can put another pie pan with some rice in it inside the crust (or use pie weights). Bake at 450°. 10 - 12 minutes. Cool.

For Filling

Cream butter and gradually add sugar, creaming well. Blend in cooled chocolate and vanilla. Add eggs one at a time, beating 5 minutes after each addition. Use medium speed. Turn into cooled pie shell. Chill 1 - 2 hours. Top with whipped cream and walnuts, if desired. To make a 9 inch pie, make 1 ½ recipes of filling.

Serves 8.

Frozen Mint Frango

A nice dessert for a ladies' luncheon.

1 cup butter
2 cups powdered sugar
4 squares semisweet chocolate, melted
4 eggs
¼ tsp. mint extract
2 tsp. vanilla
1 ½ cups vanilla wafer crumbs or graham cracker crumbs
Whipped cream
Cherries

Beat butter and sugar until fluffy. Add chocolate and beat until well blended. Add eggs, one at a time, beating after each, until fluffy. Beat in both extracts. Using the crumbs, sprinkle into paper or foil muffin cups enough to cover bottom. Add a dollop of chocolate mixture and more crumbs on top. Freeze. Serve on a plate covered with a lace doily. Top each with whipped cream and a cherry.

Serves 16 - 18.

Frozen Mocha Toffee Dessert

8 ladyfingers, split
2 tbsp. instant coffee crystals
1 tbsp. boiling water
1 qt. to ½ gallon vanilla ice cream, softened
4 (5oz.) chocolate covered toffee bars, frozen and crushed
½ cup whipping cream
2 tbsp. white crème de cacao

Line the bottom and 2 inches up the sides of an 8 inch spring form pan with the split ladyfingers, cutting to fit. Dissolve coffee in boiling water. Cool. Stir together coffee, ice cream and crushed candy. Spoon into spring form pan. Cover and freeze. Before serving, combine cream and crème de cacao and whip to soft peaks. Spread over top. Garnish with additional crushed candy.

Serves 8 - 10.

Golden Wine Cake

Cake

1 pkg. Duncan Hines yellow cake mix
1 pkg. Jell-O vanilla instant pudding mix
¾ cup oil
¾ cup white Port wine
4 eggs
1 tsp. nutmeg
Dash of salt

Frosting

⅛ tsp. nutmeg
1 cup powdered sugar
1 tsp. soft butter
Port wine (to thin)

For Cake

Put all of the above in a mixing bowl and beat 4 minutes. Put in a greased and floured HEAVY bundt pan. Bake at 350º for 45 - 50 minutes or until done.

For Frosting

After cake is out of pan and still warm, mix together nutmeg, powdered sugar, soft butter and some port wine to thin.
Heat enough to make it liquid and pour over cake as frosting.

Serves 12 - 16.

Lemon Fluff

1 cup milk
1 cup whipping cream
1 cup sugar
8 large lemons for shells
2 lemons for rind and juice

Stir milk, cream and sugar until dissolved. Pour into freezer tray or shallow pan and freeze until mushy. Add grated rind and juice of 2 lemons. Beat well. Freeze 2 hours and beat again, thoroughly, and return to freezer. When serving, remove flesh from lemons and make lemon shells. Fill shells with frozen mixture and garnish with mint leaf. Do not double recipe.

Serves 8.

Lemon Glazed Cheese Cake

This is a very showy dessert to serve for company or to take to a potluck. It looks complicated, but is well worth the effort.
See next page for glaze.

Crust

2 cups graham cracker crumbs
6 tbsp. melted butter
2 tbsp. sugar

Combine and press into a buttered 9 inch spring form pan.
Bake at 350º for 5 minutes. Cool.

Filling

3 (8 oz.)pkgs. cream cheese
¾ cup sugar
3 eggs
¼ cup lemon juice
2 tsp. grated lemon rind
2 tsp. vanilla

Beat cheese until soft. Add sugar and blend. Add eggs one at a time, beating well after each addition. Mix in lemon juice, rind and vanilla. Blend well. Turn into graham cracker crust. Bake 35 minutes. While cake is baking, make topping.

Topping

2 cups sour cream
3 tbsp. sugar
1 tsp. vanilla

After cake has baked at 350º for 35 minutes, remove from oven and gently spread on topping. Return to oven for 12 minutes. Cool on rack 30 minutes.

Lemon glaze
½ cup sugar
1 ½ tbsp. cornstarch
¼ tsp. salt
¾ cup water
⅓ cup lemon juice
1 egg yolk
1 tbsp. butter
1 tsp. grated lemon rind

In a heavy pan mix sugar, cornstarch and salt. In a separate container, combine water, lemon juice and egg yolk. Add to sugar mixture. Cook over low heat, stirring constantly until mix comes to a slow boil and is thickened. Add butter and lemon rind. Allow to cool slightly. Spread on cheesecake before glaze sets. Refrigerate.

Serves 16 - 20.

Mile High Strawberry Pie

2 egg whites
⅔ cup sugar
1 (10 oz.) pkg. frozen strawberries, partially thawed
1 tbsp. fresh lemon juice
⅛ tsp. salt
1 (13 oz.) bag Pecan Sandies cookies, crushed
½ tsp. vanilla
½ cup whipping cream, whipped

Put first five ingredients in a bowl and beat until stiff peaks form. In separate bowl, whip ½ cup cream and add the vanilla. Fold this into strawberry mixture. Pile into 10 inch pie plate lined with crushed Pecan Sandies. Freeze. When ready to serve, top each piece with whipped cream and add a strawberry, if desired.

Serves 8.

Mother's Apple Pie

1 or 2 (9 inch) pie crusts
1 cup sugar
⅓ cup orange juice
2 tbsp. flour
⅓ cup butter, melted
1 tsp. cinnamon
½ tsp. nutmeg
4 - 5 cups apples, peeled and sliced

Mix together sugar, orange juice, flour, butter, cinnamon and nutmeg. Add apples and stir to coat. Pile into piecrust and add top crust, if desired. If using a double crust, brush top with a little cream and sprinkle with sugar before baking. Bake at 400° for 20 minutes and at 350° for an additional 40 minutes.

Peach Cream Pie

A delicious summer dessert to serve when fresh peaches are in season.

1 (9 inch) pie crust
6 ripe peaches, peeled and sliced
Sugar
Cinnamon

Cream mixture:
1 cup sugar
⅓ cup flour (scant)
¼ tsp. salt
½ tsp. cinnamon
1 cup cream or half and half

Line a 9 inch pie plate with pastry. Slice peaches into pie crust and sprinkle with a little sugar and cinnamon. Mix ingredients for cream and pour over peaches. Bake at 400° for 20 minutes and then at 350° for 15 - 20 minutes more.

Serves 6 - 8.

Pecan Pie

3 eggs
¾ cup sugar
¼ lb. butter or margarine, melted
1 cup dark corn syrup
1 cup pecan halves
1 (9 inch) unbaked pie shell
Whipped cream

Beat eggs until light. Add sugar, butter and syrup, gradually beating each until well blended. Pour into unbaked pie shell and bake in 425° oven for 10 minutes. Reduce heat to 350° and bake for 30 minutes. Remove pie and cover with pecan halves and return to oven to bake 10 - 15 minutes longer or until firm. Serve warm with whipped cream.

Serves 8 - 10.

Perfect Pastry, never fails!

½ lb. butter
1 (8 oz.) pkg. cream cheese
2 cups flour

Mix all in food processor until a ball is formed. Wrap in plastic wrap or wax paper and chill for an hour or more. Will keep well in refrigerator.

Makes 2 crusts.

Pumpkin Dessert

1 pkg. yellow cake mix, reserve 1 cup
½ cup margarine, melted
3 eggs
1 (29 oz.) can pumpkin pie mix
⅔ cup milk
¼ cup sugar
1 tsp. cinnamon
¼ cup butter
Whipped cream

Mix cake mix (reserve 1 cup for topping) with ½ cup melted margarine and 1 egg. Pat into 13 x 9 greased pan. Mix pumpkin pie mix with 2 eggs and the milk. Pour onto first layer. Using the reserved cake mix, add the sugar and the cinnamon. Cut in butter with pastry blender or fork. Sprinkle over top. Bake at 350º for 45 minutes. Serve with whipped cream.

Serves 12.

Pumpkin-Mince "Peace Pie"

A delicious combination of of pumpkin and mincemeat for a holiday dessert!

1 (9 inch) unbaked pie shell
2 cups canned pumpkin
1 (14 oz.) can sweetened condensed milk
2 eggs, slightly beaten
1 tsp. cinnamon
½ tsp. salt
½ tsp. nutmeg
½ tsp. ginger
1 ⅓ cups (14 oz.) dried mincemeat, reconstituted.
Whipped cream

Preheat oven at 425°. Crimp edge of pastry to stand slightly above pan. Combine eggs, pumpkin, milk and spices and mix well. Spread mincemeat on bottom of shell, top evenly with pumpkin mixture. Bake at 425° for 15 minutes. Reduce oven to 350° and continue baking 30 - 35 minutes until knife inserted 1" from edge comes out clean. Cool thoroughly before cutting. Refrigerates well and is good reheated. Serve with whipped cream.

Serves 8.

Raisin Bread Custard Pudding

Mother was famous for this dessert. It is truly comfort food.

1 tsp. vanilla
Pinch of salt
2 or 3 slices raisin cinnamon bread
3 eggs
2 cups milk, scalded
⅓ cup sugar
Cinnamon sugar
Half and half

Butter the bread and sprinkle with cinnamon sugar. Cube the bread and put into a glass casserole. Beat eggs, slightly, and add sugar and salt. Add a little of the hot milk to the egg mixture, then all the egg mixture to the milk. Blend and add the vanilla. Strain the warm milk and egg mixture into the casserole over the cubed bread. Place the casserole into another pan and add boiling water to the depth of one inch. Bake at 350º for 30 minutes or until set. Serve at room temperature with half and half, or chill if not to be served immediately.

Serves 4 - 6.

Rum Cake

Cake
1 cup chopped pecans
1 (18 ½ oz.) pkg. yellow cake mix
1 (3 ¾ oz.) pkg. instant vanilla pudding
4 eggs
½ cup vegetable oil
½ cup cold water
½ cup Bacardi dark rum
Whipping cream, whipped
Grapes

Glaze
¼ lb. butter
¼ cup water
1 cup granulated sugar
½ cup Bacardi dark rum

For Cake
Preheat oven to 325º. Grease and flour a 10 inch bundt pan. Chop the pecans and sprinkle them evenly over the bottom of the pan. Mix the cake mix, pudding, eggs, oil and water together in a mixing bowl. Stir in the ½ cup Bacardi rum. Pour the batter over the chopped pecans and bake on the middle rack of the oven for one hour at 325º.

For Glaze
While the cake is baking, melt the butter in a saucepan. Add ¼ cup water and 1 cup sugar. Boil for 5 minutes, stirring constantly.
Allow to cool and stir in ½ cup rum.

Remove the cake from the oven and set on a rack to cool. When cool, invert onto a serving plate. Prick the top of the cake with a fork and drizzle the glaze evenly over the top, allowing it to soak into the cake. Serve with whipped cream and garnish with grapes rolled in powdered sugar.

Serves 12 - 16.

Ruth's Lemon Pie

1 (14 oz.) can sweetened condensed milk.
Juice of two lemons
Rind of 1 lemon
1 cup cream, whipped
Angel food cake

Beat milk, lemon juice and rind until thick. Add whipped cream. Line a pie plate with ¼ inch thick slices of angel food cake. Put lemon mixture on top of cake slices. Refrigerate until time to serve. Can be frozen.

Serves 8.

Strawberry Shortcake

2 cups flour
2 tsp. baking powder
½ tsp. salt
⅓ cup sugar
⅓ cup butter
1 egg
¾ cup milk
Fresh strawberries
Whipping cream

Mix flour, baking powder, salt and sugar. Cut in butter. Put egg in milk and mix. Add to flour mixture and stir well. Drop onto ungreased non-stick cookie sheet to make 6 equal portions. Bake at 425º for 15 minutes or so. Serve with crushed berries and real whipped cream.

Serves 6.

Tipsy Parson

1 large angel food cake, sliced
1 pint cream, whipped
1 qt. boiled custard with bourbon to taste
¾ cup chopped pecans
1 (6 oz.) jar maraschino cherries, sliced

Boiled Custard
4 cups milk
4 eggs
¼ tsp. salt
8 tbsp. sugar
1 tsp. vanilla
bourbon to taste (optional)

To make custard, scald milk in double boiler. Beat together, slightly, the eggs, salt and sugar. Add hot milk. Mix thoroughly and return to double boiler. Cook over hot (not boiling) water, stirring constantly until mixture coats spoon. Add vanilla. When cool, add bourbon to taste. Layer cake slices, cherries, nuts, custard and whipped cream in a pretty glass bowl. Repeat layers. Chill overnight.

Serves 12.

Turtle Cake

1 (18 ½ oz.) box German chocolate cake mix
1 (14 oz.) pkg. light caramels
½ cup evaporated milk
1 ½ sticks butter
1 cup milk chocolate chips
1 cup chopped pecans

In large bowl of an electric mixer, prepare chocolate cake mix according to package instructions. Pour ½ the batter (reserve other half) into well greased and floured 9 x 13 inch baking pan. Bake at 350º for 15 minutes. Remove from oven.

While cake is baking, in medium saucepan combine caramels, evaporated milk and butter; cook over medium heat stirring occasionally, until caramels are melted. Pour mixture over baked layer of cake and smooth evenly with spatula. Sprinkle with layer of chocolate chips and top with layer of nuts. Pour remaining batter over top. Return to oven and bake an additional 20 - 25 minutes, until cake springs back when lightly touched. Remove and cool completely on wire rack. Cut into squares to serve.

Serves 12.

12

Miscellaneous

Barbecue Sauce

½ cup onion, finely chopped
2 tbsp. brown sugar
1 tbsp. paprika
1 tsp. salt
1 tsp. dry mustard
¼ tsp. chili powder
⅛ tsp. cayenne
2 tbsp. Worcestershire
¼ cup vinegar
1 cup tomato juice
¼ cup ketchup
½ cup water

Mix together and simmer for 15 minutes. Good for ribs or chicken.

Makes 1½ cups

Chocolate Sauce

Yummy!

2 squares unsweetened chocolate
9 tbsp. sugar
6 tbsp. cream
1 egg
½ tsp. vanilla

In double boiler, over low heat, melt chocolate, sugar and cream.
Add egg and beat until thick. Add vanilla. Serve over ice cream.

Makes ¾ cup.

Cranberry Currant Walnut Sauce

1 lb. fresh cranberries
1 ¼ cups sugar
1 cup red currant preserves or jelly
1 cup water
1 cup walnuts, coarsely chopped
2 tbsp. orange peel, grated

Combine cranberries, sugar, preserves and water in a large saucepan. Heat to boiling. Reduce heat and simmer, uncovered, 20 minutes. Skim foam. Remove from heat. Stir in walnuts and orange peel. Refrigerate covered, overnight.

Serve with turkey, chicken or pork.

Makes 6 cups.

Hollandaise Sauce

Delicious!

2 egg yolks
3 tbsp. lemon juice
Salt and pepper to taste
1 stick margarine

Whisk egg yolks with lemon juice and salt and pepper. Heat in top of double boiler over low heat. Cut cold margarine into 8 pieces. Add half the margarine to the pan and cook over moderately low heat, stirring constantly, with a whisk until the margarine is melted. Add the remaining margarine and cook the sauce, stirring until it is thickened. Serve immediately.

Makes ¾ cup.

Hot Curried Fruit

Perfect with ham or chicken. Also good for a morning coffee party served with muffins and beverages.

1 (16 oz.) can cling peach halves, in heavy syrup
1 (16 oz.) can pear halves, in heavy syrup
1 (13 oz.) can pineapple chunks, in juice
1 (11 oz.) can mandarin oranges
⅓ cup butter, softened
⅔ cup brown sugar
¾ tsp. curry powder
12 maraschino cherries

Drain all fruit thoroughly. Cut pears and peaches into bite size pieces. Arrange all fruit in a glass baking dish (11 x 17 or 9 x 13). Make sauce by blending other ingredients except cherries. Spread sauce over fruit. Cover and refrigerate. Allow to marinate several hours or overnight. Remove from refrigerator ½ hour before baking. Dot with cherries and bake covered at 350° for 30 minutes.

Serves 8 - 10.

Mother's Pickles

1 (1 qt.) jar dill pickles
2 cups sugar
3 tbsp. cider vinegar
1 tsp. dill seed

Drain pickles and reserve juice. Slice pickles into rounds. Combine sugar, vinegar and dill seed with juice. Mix well. Put pickle slices back in jar and add juice mixture to cover. Tighten top of jar well and turn upside down. Turn jar back and forth several times for 1 - 2 days. Store in refrigerator.

Makes 1 qt.

Mother's Tomato Apple Chutney

A condiment that is delicious with pork or beef.

12 ripe tomatoes
12 McIntosh apples
4 yellow onions
2 tbsp. salt
3 cups sugar
2 cups cider vinegar
1 tsp. ground cloves
1 tsp. cinnamon
1 tsp. black pepper

Peel and chop tomatoes, apples and onions and place in a large pot. Add rest of ingredients and bring to a boil, then lower heat to simmer and stir frequently. Cook until thick, 4 - 5 hours. Put in sterile jars and seal.

Makes 8 pints.

Sauce à la Russe

1 cup sour cream or sour half and half
1 cup mayonnaise
½ cup chili sauce
1 tbsp. A-1 sauce
1 tbsp. horseradish
½ tsp. salt
1 tbsp. grated onion
Mix all and refrigerate overnight. Delicious with fresh vegetables.

Makes 2 cups.

Scalloped Pineapple

3 eggs, well beaten
4 cups fresh bread crumbs
2 cups sugar
1 (20 oz.) can crushed pineapple in juice, not syrup
½ lb. margarine, cut into small pieces

Beat eggs until creamy. Add other ingredients. Put in lightly greased 9 x 13 pan and bake at 350° for one hour.
Serve with roast pork or ham.

Serves 6 - 8.

Swedish Mustard Sauce

1 tbsp. dry mustard
4 tbsp. sugar
2 tbsp. vinegar
1 cup sour cream

Mix mustard and sugar together adding a dash of boiling water to dissolve sugar. Add remaining ingredients and mix. Keeps a long time in refrigerator and improves with age.

Use with ham, fish, fresh green beans or as a veggie dip.

Makes 1 cup.

Tartar Sauce

½ cup mayonnaise
2 tbsp. fresh parsley leaves, minced
5 tsp. bottled sweet pickle relish
1 tbsp. minced onion
1 tbsp. celery, minced
1 tbsp. pitted green olives, minced
1 ½ tsp. Dijon mustard
1 tsp. fresh lemon juice
½ tsp. fresh tarragon, minced or to taste
Pinch of celery seeds
Cayenne or Tabasco to taste

Mix all together and refrigerate.

Makes about ¾ cup.

Recipe Index

Appetizers

Bars
- Artichoke, 1
- Mexican Fudge, 10
- Cheese Mushroom Royale, 3
- Swiss Bacon Pleasers, 16

Canapés
- Crab Canapés, 4
- Peanut Butter and Chutney, 11
- Soufflé Crackers and Triple Crème Cheese, 15

Dips
- Hot Mushroom, 9
- Mother's Dill, 10
- Priscilla's Clam Dip, 13
- Sauce Iberia, 14

Hors d'oeuvres
- Bourbon Hot Dogs, 3
- Pecan Stuffed Mushrooms, 12
- Stuffed Pea Pods, 16

Spreads
- Avocado Cream Cheese, 2
- Fantastic Stuff, 5
- Hot Artichoke, 7
- Hot Cheese, 7
- Hot Crabmeat, 8
- Zippy Beef Olive, 17

Beverages

Blended
- Ruth's Daiquiri, 13
- Strawberry Daiquiri, 15

Punch
- Artillery, 2
- Children's, 4
- Fish House, 6
- Open House, 11
- Sangria, 14
- Whiskey Cup, 17

Breads and Rolls

Breads
- Dill Beer, 161
- Parmesan Loaf, 163
- Zucchini, 167

Coffee Cakes
- Apple Nut, 157
- Blueberry, 158
- Raspberry Cream Cheese, 164

Muffins
- Blueberry, 159
- Cherry, 160
- Raisin Bran, 163

Rolls
- Orange Rolls, 162
- Popovers, 162
- Sticky Rolls, 165
- Yeast Rolls, 166

Cookies and Bars

Bars
- Apple Dream, 169
- Chocolate Peanut Butter, 172
- Cinnamon, 173
- English Toffee, 176
- Peanut Butter, 180
- Pumpkin, 182
- Rocky Road, 183-184
- Treasure Chest, 185
- Yum Yum, 186

Cookies
- Butter Pecan Turtle, 170
- Chocolate Krispie Drops, 171
- Cornflake, 174
- Cranberry Tarts, 175
- Fruit-Nut Brandy Drop, 177
- Lemon Drop, 178
- Monster, 179
- Peanut Clusters, 180
- Pecan Dreams, 181
- Tingalings, 184

Desserts

Bananas Brennan, 190
Buster Bar Dessert, 193
Cakes
Apple Dapple, 188
Apple Pudding, 189
Chocolate Cherry, 195
Chocolate-Cherry Sundae, 196
Chocolate Mousse, 197
Chocolate Pound, 198
Cranberry Christmas, 200
Golden Wine, 207
Lemon Glazed Cheese, 209-210
Rum, 217
Strawberry Shortcake, 218
Tipsy Parson, 219
Turtle, 220
Flaming Pineapple Dessert, 203
Frozen Mint Frango, 205
Frozen Mocha Toffee Dessert, 206
Lemon Fluff, 208
Pies
Banana Split, 191
Blueberry Cheesecake, 192
Candy Bar, 194
Cranberry Apple Nut, 199
Cranberry Pecan, 201
Derby, 202
French Silk Chocolate, 204
Mile High Strawberry, 211
Mother's Apple, 211
Peach Cream, 212
Pecan, 213
Perfect Pastry, 213
Pumpkin-Mince "Peace Pie", 215
Ruth's Lemon, 218
Pumpkin Dessert, 214
Raisin Bread Custard Pudding, 216

Egg Dishes

Bacon
Bacon and Egg Strata, 64
Custom Omelet, 67
Bacon, Canadian
Fancy Egg Scramble, 72
Eggs (no meat)
Easy Oven-Baked French Toast, 68
Eggs a la Suisse, 70
Savory Eggs, 74
Scrambled Eggs for a Crowd, 75
Ham
Custom Omelet, 67
Egg Soufflé, 69
Farmer's Omelet, 73
Sausage
Breakfast Casserole, 65
Eggs and Sausage Casserole, 71
Seafood
Crab Supper Quiche, 66

Fish & Sea Food

Baked Fish Fillets, 77
Basic Butter Sauce, 77
Creamed Scallops and Mushrooms, 78
Fish Vegetable Sauté, 79
Halibut Bake, 80
Hot Seafood Salad, 81
Salmon Loaf, 82
Seafood Hot Dish, 83
Shrimp and Scallops Gruyere, 85
Shrimp Curry, 84

Main Dishes

Beef
Stew, 91
Stroganoff, 92
Swiss Corned Beef Scallop, 119
Beef, ground
Barbeque Hamburgers, 88
Casserole of Layers, 93
Fu Man Chew, 103
Goulash, 104
Meat Loaf, 108
Oriental Hot Dish, 111
Shipwreck Stew, 115
Sour Cream Noodle Bake, 116
Wild Rice Company Casserole, 123
Chicken
All in One Chicken Dinner, 87
Chicken Divan, 94
Chicken Elegante, 95
Chicken Escallope, 96
Chicken in Phyllo, 97
Chicken Kiev, 98
Chicken Waikiki Beach, 99
Company Casserole, 100
Evelyn's Easy Good Chicken, 102
Hot Chicken Casserole, 105
Oriental Chicken, 110
Tasty Chicken Casserole, 121

Lamb
Roast Leg of Lamb, 114
Meatless
Macaroni and Cheese Soufflé, 107
Priscilla's Macaroni and Cheese, 113
Pasta
Italian Spaghetti Sauce, 106
Mother's Lasagna, 109
Pasta Primavera, 112
Spaghetti Pie, 117
Stuffed Shells, 118
Pork
Barbequed Country Spareribs, 89
Barbecue Sauce, 90
Country Style Pork Chops, 101

Turkey
Swiss Turkey Casserole, 120
Turkey or Ham and Wild Rice Casserole, 122

Miscellaneous
Barbeque Sauce, 222
Chocolate Sauce, 222
Cranberry Currant Walnut Sauce, 223
Hollandaise Sauce, 223
Hot Curried Fruit, 224
Mother's Pickles, 225
Mother's Tomato/Apple Chutney, 226
Sauce a la Russe, 227
Scalloped Pineapple, 227
Swedish Mustard Sauce, 228
Tartar Sauce, 228

Potatoes and Rice
Aristocratic Rice, 149
Baked Hash Brown Potatoes, 150
Baked Mashed Potatoes, 150
Deluxe Hash Browns, 151
Green Chilies and Rice Casserole, 152
Patrician Potatoes, 153
Pittsburgh Potatoes, 154
Wild Rice Casserole, 155

Salads and Salad Dressings
Chicken
Chicken, 38
Luncheon, 48
Make Ahead Chef , 49
Mandarin, 50
Oriental, 54
Summer, 58
Egg
Egg Ring, 39-40
Dressings
Colonial Inn, 39
Honey, 43
Hot Bacon, 44
Mother's Oil/Vinegar, 52
Orange Salad Dressing for Spinach Salad, 53
Sweet French, 60
Sweet Oil, 60
Thousand Island, 61
Fruit
Black Cherry Jell-O, 35
Blueberry Jell-O Mold, 35
Fresh Fruit, 41
Frozen Pineapple Cranberry, 41
Orange, 53
Ham
Luncheon, 48
Overnight Pasta, 55
Pasta
Italian, 46
Overnight Pasta, 55
Potato
Charlie's, 37
Hot Baked, 45
Mother's, 52
Seafood
Hot Seafood, 81
Molded Shrimp, 51
Shrimp, 56
Turkey
Luncheon, 48
Make Ahead Chef, 49
Vegetable
Cabbage, 36
Chef, 49
Gazpacho Relish, 42
Herbed Tomatoes, 43
Hot Bacon, 44
Lou's, 47
Luncheon, 48
Pea-Nut, 56
Spanish, 57
Superb Tossed, 59
Vegetable Bouquet, 62

Soup

Beef Vegetable, 19
Beer Cheese, 20
Carrot, 21
Cheddar Corn Chowder, 22
Cheesy Cream of Vegetable, 23
Chunky Sausage Chowder, 24
Clam Bisque, 25
Cream of Artichoke, 26
Creamy Cheddar Cheese, 27
French, 28
"Hearty", 29
Leek and Potato, 30
Mother's Split Pea, 31
Provencal Vegetable, 32
Wild Rice, 33

Vegetables and Side Dishes

Asparagus Parmesan, 125
Baked Tomatoes, 126
Baked Zucchini, 127
Cauliflower Au Gratin, 127
Cheesy Brussels Sprouts Bake, 128
Cheesy Zucchini Casserole, 129
Chinese Vegetables, 130
Creamed Onions, 131
Curried Corn Pudding, 132
Easy Rutabaga Au Gratin, 133
Fried Tomatoes, 134
Gingered Carrots, 135
Green Beans with Mushrooms, 135
Monterey Zucchini Casserole, 136
Mother's Baked Beans, 137
Noodles with Sesame Dressing, 138
Ratatouille, 139
Red Cabbage, 140
Sauteed Cherry Tomatoes, 141
Scrumptious Carrots, 141
Simmered Autumn Vegetables, 142
Spinach Artichoke Casserole, 143
Spinach Casserole, 144
Spinach Pecan Bake, 145
Stir Fried Celery and Broccoli, 146
Sunday Company Casserole, 147

Priscilla van Horne (right) lives in Grosse Pointe, Michigan with her boxer, Heidi. She is very active in her church as well as in Goodwill. She has a reputation for being an excellent cook and she also has a sweet tooth. That's why the desserts chapter is so large.

Her daughter Jen van Horne (left), lives in Minneapolis, Minnesota. She teaches English language learners in the Twin Cities. Jen worked on this book as a proof reader and she helped write the dedication.

Suellen Kruse lives on the North Shore of Lake Superior near Grand Marais, Minnesota and owns Kah-Nee-Tah, a small resort and fine art gallery in Lutsen, Minnesota. She has two male Bichons who are brothers and a female Shih Tzu named Kaila who goes to the Gallery every day.

She is active in her church and is the President of the North Shore Health Care Foundation. The foundation raises funds and makes quarterly grants to qualified health care providers in Cook County, Minnesota.

Special Thanks to the following people for all of their help in making this book possible.

Karl Hansen — computer guru
Katherine Hellner — graphic designer
Marie Sweeney — watercolor on front cover
Donna Williams — index specialist